THE DULCE WARS:

UNDERGROUND ALIEN BASES & THE BATTLE FOR PLANET EARTH

By Branton

GW00645469

INNER LIGHT/GLOBAL COMMUNICATIONS

THE DULCE WARS:
Underground Alien Bases &
The Battle For Planet Earth

● ● ● ● ● ● ● ● ● ●

Cover art © Charles Gregory
Introduction, all other new material as well as editing
and typesetting copyright 1999 © Global Communications

Special thanks to Branton for utilization of
his research and dedication to planet Earth and
its inhabitants.

==

DEDICATED TO JIM KEITH

==

ISBN: 1-892062-12-7

Timothy G. Beckley, Editorial Director
Assistant to Publisher, Carol Rodriguez
Free catalog from Global Communications,
Box 753, New Brunswick, NJ 08903
www.webufo.net
Free subscription to CONSPIRACY JOURNAL
e-mailed every week. Go to above site NOW!

The Dulce Wars

Contents

Forward By Commander X 5

Introduction 6

Chapter One
The Octopus, Black Projects and the Dulce Facility 9
Chapter Two
High Strangeness on the Archuleta Plateau 17
Chapter Three
Dulce, New Mexico and a Cosmic Conspiracy? 22
Chapter Four
Dulce, New Mexico and the Nazi Connection 40
Chapter Five
Report From a Japanese Television Crew 48
Chapter Six
Cosmic Top Secrets and the Dulce Base 58
Chapter Seven
Probing Deeper Into the Dulce Enigma 66
Chapter Eight
A Dulce Vanguard at Deep Springs? 73
Chapter Nine
An Alien Fifth Column on Earth? 82
Chapter Ten
A Deep Dark Secret at Dulce 87
Chapter Eleven
A Dulce Base Security Officer Speaks Out 91
Chapter Twelve
Paul Bennewitz - One Man Against an Empire 110
Chapter Thirteen
The Strange Life and Death of Philip Schneider 133

The Dulce Wars

Crafts in subterranean bays of S4 according to
Derek Henessy (1987) and Bob Lazar (1988-1989)

Zonnery - planet
#4 of Sirius A
system

21 May 1953, Kingman, AZ?

Jello mold

Bay ① Ø ~ 9m, hatch ~ 1 x 0.7m

Bay ② Ø ~ 9m

Bay ③ was disassembled when Lazar was in S4?

Bay ④ was disassembled when Lazar was in S4?

Observed in flight
26 February 1951 over
Tikaboo, emanating red-orange
and yellow light
Cake tin

Outlook from the top

Sign on the hull?

Bay ⑤ Ø ~ 12m?

Big hat

Bay ⑥ Ø ~ 18m

Was disassembled when Lazar was in S4?

Bay ⑦ Ø ~ 6.5m?   There were 7 disks only in S4 in 1987

Transported to S4 in 1987 or 1988
Sport model

Bay ⑧ Ø ~ 10.5m, h ~ 4.5m, crew 3 EBEs

Crashed in August 1981, transported to S4 ~ in
(was also on the posters in S4)   1987
Floor model

Bay ⑨ Ø ~ 10 - 11 m. Damaged
(holes in the bottom and hull   9 different disks, according to Bob Lazar

Illustration by Anton Anfalow

The Dulce Wars

FORWARD
By Commander X

In the early 1970's I began to hear disturbing rumors concerning the secret of UFOs and an extraterrestrial presence based at various locations on our planet. In my position as a military intelligence operative, I have been privy to all sorts of unusual secrets and wild, reckless "scientific" experiments, all conducted in the name of national security. While no one came right out and said to me: "You are working with acquired alien technology." There were times when it was covertly implied that black project experiments were being conducted on just such items. How this technology was received was never explained.

At the time I didn't take much stock in such wild stories. After all, in my line of work, there is no such thing as the truth. Information is deliberately seeded with "disinformation" to prevent anyone but a few at the very top from ever knowing the full story. Besides, I knew for a fact that the military and National Intelligence Agencies had been using UFOs and their alleged alien pilots as covers for top secret operations. These campaigns ranged from disguising spy planes to seeing how quickly a wild rumor can be spread by word of mouth. I soon learned that there is really no such thing as the truth.

The book you are about to read was compiled by the mysterious Branton, who, because of the potentially damaging information that he has uncovered, chooses to remain anonymous. Even though many UFO investigators began reporting these same stories in the late 1980s and early 1990s, much of the information gathered by Branton for this book has never been published before.

I have been asked at times whether I can confirm any of the unsettling information concerning secret alien bases and an unholy alliance between world governments and extraterrestrial visitors. While in the past, I too was told almost the very same stories (years before they began to circulate among the UFO community). I must hedge my bets and say that I can neither confirm or deny the validity of such tales. A part of me would like to think that these stories are merely some kind of disinformation campaign being played out by hidden controllers with some unknown purpose in mind. However, in the back of my mind there does exist the fear that this could all be true. That alien races with their own unsavory agenda have established hidden, underground strongholds among us. You must decide for yourself what is fiction and what is fact.

The Dulce Wars

Introduction

For several decades, researchers of "paranormal phenomena" have devoted themselves to specialized fields of "fringe scientific" investigation. Some of these various fields of 'borderline' research -- which have surfaced in order to document or attempt to explain a wide divergence of phenomena -- have included:

Aerial or UFO phenomena, Psychic or Psychotronic investigation, Cattle and Animal Mutilations, Vampirism, Men-In-Black, Conspiracies and Assassinations, Secret Societies, Underground Anomalies, Quantum Mechanics, Legends and Mythology, Ancient Civilizations, the 'Mothmen' and other 'Crypto-Zoological' encounters, Energy Grids and other Geo-Magnetic anomalies, Biogenetics and Cloning, Cybernetics and Artificial Intelligence, Abductions and Missing Time, Hypnotherapy and Mind Control, Missing Persons... There are no doubt many others that I have not mentioned.

In the 1950's, experts in some of these areas of investigation began hearing the first faint hints that 'something' was going on in the American southwest, near the "Four Corners" region of the United States. First these hints and rumors were brief, vague and confusing, yet they sparked enough interest to provoke further investigations as the years passed.

At first these fringe scientists who concerned themselves with the mysteries and anomalies of this region began raising more questions than answers, as they continued to probe into an 'enigma' which seemed to eventually focus itself in and around a small desert town lost amidst the mesas of northwestern New Mexico.

In the late 1970's and early 1980's, the mystery – and subsequently the interest – deepened as reports began to slowly emanate from the area suggesting that something significant and horrifying had taken place there, near the small town of Dulce [pronounced "dul-see"], New Mexico. The many different phenomena, those previously mentioned, seemed for some strange reason to converge and coagulate into one vast enigmatic scenario of high strangeness in and around this seemingly insignificant and small New Mexican town. Researchers commenced to analyze and categorize their respective phenomena, looking for patterns and concentrations, and came to the realization that several of these phenomena apparently converged in the American southwest. . . the charts showed the largest concentrations of UFO sightings – Northwestern New Mexico; the epicenter of Cattle Mutilation Phenomena - Northwestern New Mexico. Other experts in their fields began to find similar patterns merging and linking with other phenomena at underlying levels. Researchers into Conspiracies, Secret Societies, Underground Anomalies, Legends and Mythology, Ancient Civilizations, Energy Grids, Geo-Magnetic anomalies, Biogenetics, Abductions and Missing Time, Missing Persons and investigators of other specialized 'vanguard' fields of research began looking toward this small desert town. These unusual convergence's of phenomena in a singular locale sparked even more interest and investigation.

From that point on, it was as if some ancient seal had been broken, as if an ancient cloud of darkness had begun imploding in upon itself, broken apart by the piercing light of human perception and the relentless probing's and scrutiny of brave and daring souls.

Sensing that something very wrong and unnatural was going on here, something ancient and evil, some of these brave souls – who by choice or chance found themselves battling-it-out on the front lines against ancient forces that were determined to keep themselves from being exposed – continued to wage their all-too-often personal battles against the enigma. . . some of these inevitably losing their minds if not their very lives in the process.

As these brave souls were worn down by the intensity of this psychic warfare in their efforts to expose and defeat this "mystery of iniquity" [to coin a Biblical phrase], they sent out desperate calls for reinforcements. Many answered the call, and the ancient and formerly invisible beast that had managed to hide itself below the deserts of the southwest like a dragon in its lair, began to stir in rage and terror at these new exposures, and to lash back at its new-found enemies.

The repercussions began to be felt throughout the whole country, through which the beast had reached out its deadly tentacles – which were also in the process of being exposed along with the black heart of the beast itself.

The walls of the ancient fortress concealing the beast or the enigma began to crumble and fall with increasing intensity. From the murky blackness within, a faint collective cry was heard as if from another world – the voices of multitudes who were desperately calling out for help to the only ones who could hear them, those who were beginning to see yet had not yet become the slaves of the enigma itself. Many of us who have continued the battle have sacrificed our comfort, our social and economic welfare, and in some cases even our very lives to fight the Enigma, because we have caught a brief glimpse of the potential threat that "the enemy within" poses to the future of Liberty and to this great Independent nation of America.

What you will see throughout these pages is the collective results of our efforts and – I'm not ashamed to say – the results of more than a little Divine Intervention as well. Many of us, such as yours truly, have been 'victimized' by the enigma for the greater part of our lives, and have decided that the only way to be 'free' from its grasp is to practice the old military rule: "The best Defense is a good Offense. . ."

So there you have it. Like those before us, we send this work forth as a warning and a call to arms, to others who value truth and freedom. For those who may not believe everything that follows, I challenge you to become personally involved [however using caution in the event that these collective reports DO turn out to be true] and PROVE the claims made herein point-by-point, one way or another.

Much of the information in this volume is of an incredible and, some might say, an unbelievable nature. I have decided NOT to hold back ANY information or claims regarding the Dulce enigma and related scenarios, the reason for this being that underground or earth-based anomalies are always there for anyone who is interested or daring enough to probe and investigate.

Throughout this volume I have nevertheless offered my own 'opinions' and 'perspectives' based on circumstantial evidence [two or more reports from different sources which relay identical themes, and so on]. These admittedly are my own opinions and can be received or discarded according to the readers own perceptions in regards to the nature of reality. I have formed these opinions based on my own perceptions of the overall data, and since these are my perceptions, they are not infallible but are subject to change or revision with the revelation of new information. The reader is free to form his or her own conclusions and opinions based on the accumulated data, just as I have done.

Branton

The Dulce Wars

Chapter One
The Octopus, Black Projects and the Dulce Facility

The following article comes from the *TC TECHNICAL CONSULTANT*, Nov.-Dec., 1991 issue:

"The death of a journalist in West Virginia, plus the jailing of an alleged CIA computer consultant in Washington State may be elements of a much wider scandal that could have serious implications. . .

"What started out as an investigation of an apparent case of pirated software has grown to be a project involving hundreds of journalists all over the world.

"The dead journalist, Joseph Daniel 'Danny' Casolaro was found dead August 10th in a motel room in West Virginia. His wrists were slashed seven times on each wrist and a suicide note was found nearby. The only manuscript of his book, with accompanying notes, WAS MISSING.

"The book, provisionally titled 'The Octopus', was meant to be an explosive expose of misdeeds by the Justice Department under the Reagan administration. *Time Magazine* also reported that Casolaro's research centered on gambling and attempted arms deals at the Cabazon reservation near Indio [California].

"Indeed, the scope of Casolaro's investigation was so large that any one of a large number of areas of research could have been the trigger for a possible hit.

"While authorities declared his death a suicide, his relatives definitely stated that Casolaro's mental state was sound, indeed upbeat, after the completion of his book.

"Casolaro started his work nearly two years before, investigating the bankrupting of a small computer software company called Inslaw, allegedly by the U.S. Justice Department. INSLAW, a company headed by Bill and Nancy Hamilton of Washington D.C., (no connection to researcher Bill Hamilton, whose writings on the Dulce enigma appear later in this volume. - **Branton**) had developed a package known as PROMIS -- short for Prosecutor's Management Information System -- to act as a case management tool for the Justice Department's unwieldy work load. Inslaw President Bill Hamilton has claimed that Ed Meese associate EARL BRIAN was given control of pirated versions of the PROMIS software by Meese to sell back to different U.S. government agencies for great profit. Two courts have so far agreed with Hamilton, awarding an 8 million dollar judgment, but a higher ('Justice Dept.'? - Branton) court of appeal has quashed the award and the verdict, declaring that it was not the jurisdiction of the lower courts. As of October 9, the case has moved into the realm of the Supreme Court.

"EARL BRIAN OWNS UNITED PRESS INTERNATIONAL [UPI] and FINANCIAL NEWS NETWORK [FNN].

"According to a Washington man, who claims to have modified the cobol-based software for the CIA and other intelligence agencies, the software was a reward for Earl Brian's role in arranging the so-called 'October Surprise' gambit, the alleged conspiracy to withhold the American hostages in Iran until after the 1980 election which saw Carter removed from power. The 'October Surprise' scandal has taken some time to emerge.

"In a Paris meeting, President Bush is alleged to have met with Ali Akabar Hashemi Rafsanjani, the speaker of the Iranian Parliament, Mohammed Ali Rajai, the future President of Iran and Manucher Ghorbanifar, an Iranian arms dealer with connections to Mossad, according to Navy Captain Gunther Russbacher who claims to have flown Bush, William Casey – the CIA chief – and Donald Gregg, a CIA operative to that location. Russbacher, who made these allegations in May is now in jail on Terminal Island, convicted on the charge of impersonating a U.S. Attorney.

(Note: Russbacher 'defected' from the CIA with 12 Navy Seals under his command, and was on at least two occasions the target of attempted CIA hits. The would-be assassins attempted to drive Gunther and his wife off of roads and down the side-cliffs to their deaths, however according to Russbacher his SEAL-team agents who were watching over him unbeknownst to the intended assassins, moved up quickly from behind and sent the CIA "hit men" to THEIR deaths instead. - **Branton**)

"The Washington man is MICHAEL RICONOSCIUTO who is now waiting for a trial in a Washington jail on conspiracy to sell drugs charges, charges which Riconosciuto claims are manufactured. Indeed, the charge made against

Riconosciuto were made one week after Riconosciuto authored and signed an affidavit describing his role in modifying the pirated software.

(Note: It is interesting what connections we can find here. Michael Riconosciuto was a Wackenhut-CIA employee who told researcher Michael Lindemann that he had attempted to get a whole helicopter full of documents and evidence detailing illegal biogenetic activities and non-Congressionally sanctioned projects involving 'illegal aliens' out of the Nevada Test Site. The chopper was blown out of the sky, killing all five personnel on board.

Michael's father happened to be Marshall Riconosciuto, a fascist and a supporter of Adolph Hitler who was a very close friend of Fred L. Crisman. Crisman was involved in the Maurey Island 'UFO' sighting incident in 1947 near Tacoma, Washington, which researcher Anthony Kimory believes involved the test-flight of hybrid CIA - PROJECT PAPERCLIP - NAZI aerial disks.

There are several sources which claim that by the early 1940's the Nazis had succeeded in test-flying wingless lenticular craft powered by rotary devices, rocket power, and DONUT CONFIGURATION jet turbine engines – rather than cylindrical – with the cabin stabilized by gyro, the compressors rotating in one direction and the expansion chambers and vectored exhausts rotating in the opposite direction.

After the war had ended several of the Nazi scientists who WERE captured and who had helped to develop the revolutionary aircraft – were recruited by the CIA as a result of a secret deal that had been made between Allen Dulles, a member of the Bavarian Illuminati; and Nazi S.S. General Reinhard Gehlen, a member of the Bavarian Thule Society. The deep connections between the Bavarian Illuminati which sponsored the CIA and the Bavarian Thule society which sponsored the Nazis allowed for the upper covert-ops levels of the CIA to be manned by nothing less than the core of the Nazi S.S. itself, with the help of fascist sympathizers and fifth column double-agents working within American intelligence, although some leading Nazis were 'sacrificed' to the Nuremberg trials to appease the Allies and establish the illusion that Europe had been de-Nazified.

Fred L. Crisman incidentally was a 'witness' to the Maurey Island event and had helped two Army G-2 agents acquire 'slag samples' which fell from one of the six DONUT-SHAPED ships observed. On their way to deliver the samples to Wright-Patterson AFB in Ohio, their plane crashed and both G-2 agents were killed. Some people at the time insisted that the plane had been sabotaged. Two of the reporters who investigated the incident lost their lives, and Kenneth Arnold who investigated the incident after being commissioned by *AMAZING STORIES* editor Ray Palmer, claimed that his conversations with a high Air Force official concerning the subject were electronically monitored. Also, strange government agents in dark suits were seen in the area.

Shortly after his investigation Kenneth Arnold, during an air-search for a crashed plane over Mt. Rainier, saw 9 crescent-shaped discs which he called flying saucers. The news media publicized the incident and the term stuck and became a media catch word ever since. Also around this same time – 1947 – Arnold escaped a near-fatal crash when his airplane mysteriously lost power. The connections do not end here.

Fred L. Crisman was a close friend to Clay Shaw, whom Louisiana District Attorney James Garrison – see the movie *JFK* – accused of being the CIA-Mafia go-between in the John F. Kennedy murder. Garrison arrested Shaw in an effort to charge him and the CIA with the JFK assassination, however only a few days before the hearing Garrison's star witness David Ferry was killed, and Garrison's remaining evidence was not enough to bring about a conviction.

Fred Crisman was the first man Clay Shaw called when he heard that Garrison intended to implicate him. Garrison also believed that Clay Shaw himself was involved with PROJECT PAPERCLIP, the secret operation to bring Nazi war criminals into the United States by the hundreds – some say thousands – and give them immunity and new identities in such institutions as U.S. Intelligence, the Military-Industrial complex, the Space agencies, and the various Rockefeller-connected oil cartels such as ARCO, STANDARD [EXXON], ZAPATA, etc., corporations that were supported by the Bavarian-based secret-society lodges, corporations that had actually sold oil to the Nazis during World War II and helped keep the Nazi "war machine" operating.

According to Garrison, Crisman worked as a middle-man between the fascist policy makers and the lower echelons of the Military-Industrial Complex. (For the complete story about Operation Paperclip and the underground UFO bases of Hitler's elite scientific corps, read: *Evil Agenda of the Secret Government*, by Tim Swartz - 1999 Global Communications.- **Branton**)

"The affidavit also claimed that he [Michael Riconosciuto], had been contacted by phone and threatened by PETER VIDENIEKS – a Justice Department employee and Customs official who Riconosciuto alleged had intelligence ties – as to the possible consequences of his going public with certain information.

"According to Riconosciuto, Videnieks was a frequent visitor to the Cabazon Indian reservation near Palm Springs and visited with tribal manager, John P. Nichols. Nichols was in essence Riconosciuto's boss in a number of enterprises conducted on reservation land and the PROMIS modification was just one of these projects. According to Riconosciuto, in an interview with T.C. conducted from jail, the PROMIS software was modified to install a backdoor access for use by American intelligence services. The software was then sold to 88 different countries as a sort of 'Trojan horse' package enabling us to access their intelligence systems. According to Riconosciuto these countries included Iraq and Libya.

"Correspondence between Nichols and other companies, if authentic, indicates that Riconosciuto's claims of his expertise in the area of electronics and armaments appear to be true. Marshall Riconoscuito, Michael's father, is a reputed former business partner of Richard Nixon.

"According to Riconosciuto, the fuzzy status of reservation land as 'sovereign' allowed elements of the CIA and organized crime to conduct business uniquely.

"Among the projects worked on during this time were joint projects with WACKENHUT, a company loaded with former CIA and NSA personnel and business ventures with the Saudi Arabian royal family and other unusual projects.

"A joint venture with Southern California Edison will soon be generating power for bio-mass drawn from local waste outlets. Biological warfare projects were investigated with Stormont laboratories looking into the creation of 'pathogenic viruses' and enhanced fuel-air explosive weapons were created and tested in league with Meridian Arms at the NEVADA TESTING RANGE which matched the explosive power of nuclear devices. These enhanced weapons gained their power from polarizing the molecules in the gas cloud by modification of the electric field, a technology developed from exploring Thomas Townsend Brown's suppressed work.

The Dulce Wars

"Riconosciuto is said to have worked on the enhanced fuel-air explosive weapons with Gerald Bull of Space Research Corporation. Bull, now deceased, later became an arms advisor to Saddam Hussein. It is said that HUSSEIN POSSESSES THE FAE TECHNOLOGY.

"In July, Anson Ng, a reporter for the Financial Times of London was shot and killed in Guatemala. He had reportedly been trying to interview an American there named Jimmy Hughes, a one-time director of security for the Cabazon Indian Reservation secret projects.

"In April, a Philadelphia attorney named Dennis Eisman was found dead, killed by a single bullet in his chest. According to a former federal official who worked with Eisman, the attorney was found dead in the parking lot where he had been due to meet with a woman who had crucial evidence to share substantiating Riconosciuto's claims. Both Eisman's and Ng's deaths were declared suicides by authorities.

"Fred Alvarez, a Cabazon tribal leader who was in vocal opposition to the developments on the reservation, was found shot to death WITH two friends in 1981. Their murder remains unsolved.

"The leader of the House, Thomas Foley, announced last month that a formal inquiry will be initiated into the Inslaw case. Foley appointed Senator Terry Sanford as co-chairman of the joint congressional panel. Prior to his election, Senator Sanford was the attorney REPRESENTING Earl Brian in his 1985 takeover bid for United Press International and was instrumental in appointing Earl Brian, a medical doctor, to the board of Duke Medical School, of which Sanford is President.

"However, despite repeated requests from journalists to produce photographs showing Riconosciuto together with Brian, and requests to produce his passport showing his alleged trip to Iran, he has not yet done so. Also Riconosciuto failed to be able to describe Peter Videnieks to CNN's Moneyline program, claiming a medical condition prevented him from remembering clearly.

"This led one former intelligence operative to speculate that we may be witnessing a very sophisticated intelligence operation being played out in public.

"Former F.B.I. Special Agent, Ted Gunderson, speaks FOR Riconosciuto's credibility. Gunderson, who lives in Manhattan Beach, has worked with Riconosciuto for many years in his capacity as private investigator.

"Together, according to Gunderson, they were responsible for thwarting a terrorist operation during the Los Angeles Olympics. According to Gunderson, Riconosciuto was well known in certain circles as a genius in almost all sciences.

"The so-called drug operation broken up in Washington State was an electrohydrodynamic mining operation claimed Gunderson, using Townsend Brown technology. A videotape viewed by this journalist revealed metallic powders and apparent processes unrelated to drug manufacture. Indeed, a government analysis of soil samples revealed the absence of drug contamination, but a high concentration of barium. Barium is often found in high voltage related work.

"Unsubstantiated information from an intelligence source claims that the current situation is THE VISIBLE EFFECT OF A WAR CURRENTLY GOING ON IN THE INTELLIGENCE COMMUNITY between a group centered in the CIA called AQUARIUS [around a powerful center known as MJ-12] and a group known as COM-12 centered around Naval Intelligence. COM-12 is reputedly trying to sustain a rearguard action to sustain and preserve constitutional government and is deliberately LEAKING INFORMATION damaging to the former group."

In the same publication, same issue, there appeared a follow-up article just following the one given above. Written by Thomas Zed, the article, titled ***WACKENHUT'S CONNECTION WITH THE BLACK PROJECT WORLD***, stated: "The Wackenhut company has a very close connection to the world of BLACK BUDGET PROJECTS. Besides being connected with the Cabazon venture mentioned in this issue it is also responsible, according to jailed computer consultant Michael Riconosciuto, FOR THE SECRET PROJECTS BEING UNDERTAKEN IN DULCE, NEW MEXICO where the JICARILLA INDIAN RESERVATION IS BEING SIMILARLY USED.

"After sending two of my colleagues there recently AND RECEIVING CONFIRMATION THAT THERE WAS A TOP SECRET MILITARY TYPE INSTALLATION, I decided to call the newspaper office and make an educated bluff.

"I identified myself as a freelance reporter from Los Angeles – and told the newspaper that I was doing a story on the Cabazon reservation biological warfare projects that had been undertaken there on behalf of the CIA. I told her that I had heard that there were similar things being done in Dulce and would like to know what was going on.

"The official I spoke to BECAME FRIGHTENED and said, 'I can't talk to you about that! It would be very unprofessional of me to talk to you about that. You'll have to speak to the President of the tribe.' She then hung up.

"I have yet to call back and ask the President of the tribe, but will report on that in the next issue.

"Wackenhut is also responsible for security of a lot of UNDERGROUND FACILITIES in California and Nevada, including the notorious S-4 or AREA 51 in Nevada where Townsend Brown flying disk technology [written about in a T.C. recent issue] has been flying and developing for decades.

"A recent helicopter crash at the area, where two pilots and three security guards from Wackenhut flying in a Messerschmit BO-105 helicopter were killed was not at all accidental claimed Riconosciuto, who said that the individuals aboard the helicopter were traveling with sensitive documents. Groups are now investigating Riconosciuto's claims. . ."

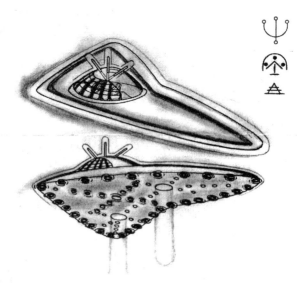

In 1947, Kenneth Arnold, during an air-search for a crashed plane over Mt. Rainier, saw 9 crescent-shaped discs which he called flying saucers. The news media publicized the incident and the term stuck and quickly became a media catch word.

Chapter Two
High Strangeness on the Archuleta Plateau

In the Spring of 1990 researcher Jason Bishop sent copies of the following report to a select few investigators, and later gave permission for the report to be distributed among a wider readership. Is the object described within the report the product of secret technology being developed by the Military-Industrial Complex as part of some covert or deep-cover space project? Or does it involve something a bit more 'alien' than mere top secret black-project research and top-of-the-line vanguard aircraft designs – the Stealth series, the Aurora, etc. – which are being developed at the Nevada Test Site? Or, could it be a combination of both?

The transcript, titled: 'RECOLLECTIONS AND IMPRESSIONS OF VISIT TO DULCE, NEW MEXICO - OCTOBER 23, 24, 1988', is reproduced in its entirety below.

"Upon arrival I was introduced to Dr. John F. Gille, a French National. Dr. Gille has a PhD in Math/Physics from the University of Paris. He had worked very closely with the French Government on the UFO phenomena in that country. (Side Note: Dr. Gille had also released a report on another Dulce-like base near Pine Gap - Alice Springs, Australia. This base is a massive multi-levelled facility run by the 'Club of Rome' which, like the 'Bildeberger' organization, is reputedly a cover for the Bavarian Illuminati.

The article spoke of antigravity disk research, and plans to make Pine Gap a major "control center" for a "New World Order". Pine Gap is equipped with whole levels of computer terminals tied-in to the major computer mainframes of the world which contain the intimate details of most of the inhabitants of industrialized nations.

The article also spoke of the infiltration of several major religious denominations, the media, international governments, the economy, education, and other levels of society by the Bavarian Illuminati, in order to prepare the way for a New World Order dictatorship. The report also stated that the workers at Pine Gap are highly indoctrinated and programmed so that they do not threaten or sabotage the security of the Illuminati projects being carried out there. - **Branton**).

The Dulce Wars

"He told me," Bishop continues, "that he has not worked in his chosen field for fifteen years, having devoted all of his time to research on UFOs. Dr. Gille is an amiable, forthright man. He has no reservations about expressing his own views on the subject. He does hold several beliefs that border on the paranormal. Dr. Gille had his wife, Elaine, with him. My personal view of him is one of caution. Until I get to know him better, I feel that I should be very careful.

"Edmound Gomez is a rancher. His ranch is 13 miles west of Dulce. (Note: Accounts given by others state that the ranch is 13 miles east of Dulce, however whatever the case may be it's safe to say that the ranch is 13 miles FROM Dulce. **Branton**).

"From 1975 until 1983 the Gomez ranch was the scene [epicenter] of most of the cattle mutilations that took place in the northern New Mexico / southern Colorado area. He told me that his family homesteaded the Dulce area 111 years ago and that as a result of these mutilations, they lost $100,000 in cattle over an eight year period. One of these cases occurred only 200 yards behind his home. He showed me the area.

"Edmound was very open and discussed with me the various mutilation cases that had occurred on his ranch and on those of others. Upon our return from the mountain trip, he invited me to his home where he shared with me various photographs, clippings, letters etc. relating to the cases. He loaned me several overhead photographs of the Mt. Archuleta area. I hope to be able to have them examined through image intensification techniques.

"Edmound also told me about the many times that combat ready troops had been spotted in the area. Some of these troops were found in areas that are only gotten to through four-wheel drive trucks or on foot. [This is VERY rugged country]. The troops were also spotted in areas that only the Apache has permission to go. When the reported 'experimental aircraft' went down in 1983, there were 'hundreds of troops, armed to the teeth' reported in the area. When approached, the troops would run and disappear.

"Participants in the Mt. Archuleta expedition were: Gabe Valdez, Edmound Gomez, Dr. John Gille, Manuel Gomez [Edmound's brother], Jeff and Matt Valdez [Gabe's sons]. Because of Gabe's position as head of the State Police in Dulce and Edmound being a part of the community, we were given permission to go onto the mountain. It is located on the Apache Reservation.

"We left about 1430 hrs, Sunday, 23 October 1988. We used Gabe's four wheel drive pickup truck to get up the mountain. The road was incredibly difficult. At one time we had to dig out the side of the mountain in order to allow the truck to pass. At about 1730 hrs we arrived at the proposed campsite. It was on a relatively flat area about 300 yards from the peak of Mt. Archuleta.

"Gabe and Edmound both told me that in 1978 there was an agreement between the Ute Indians [Colorado] and the Federal Government. This agreement consisted of the Ute Nation receiving all the territory now occupied along the New Mexico/Colorado border with the explicit agreement that they would strictly enforce a 'NO TRESPASSING' regulation along the border of their territory. Therefore, it is not possible to even cross the Ute Reservation without special permission from the Tribal Headquarters. If caught without this permission you are liable for a fine and/or jail and expulsion. There is now a road leading to the Archuleta area through the reservation. It is patrolled by the Indian Forest Service.

(Note: the Colorado border is only a relatively few miles away from and to the north of the Archuleta plateau. - **Branton**).

"At 1951 hrs. all seven of us spotted a very bright light coming from the northwest at a very high rate of speed. The object appeared to be boomerang shaped with a very bright light just below its center (Some have alleged that these 'boomerang' shaped vehicles may have some connection with a super-secret black budget space operation called Alternative-3. - **Branton**). The light was a bright white, blue and green. As it approached, it slowed down [obviously under intelligent control], seemed to reverse direction, finally stopping. When it stopped, a shower of what appeared to be sparks were emitted from each end of the boomerang, and then it began moving forward again and disappeared from sight at a very high rate of speed. All this took place in approximately 10 to 15 seconds. We attempted to take a picture of the object but were unsuccessful.

"About 2200 hours we climbed to the summit of Mt. Archuleta and watched for about an hour and a half. We could see across the canyon in the moonlight. This canyon wall is where Paul Bennewitz [prominent and well known physicist and UFO investigator] claimed an 'alien' base is located and that during the night their ships are seen entering and leaving cave openings in the cliff wall.

The Dulce Wars

"During our stay on the peak, we saw two very bright lights on the cliff walls in the exact location where Paul said the base openings were. There are no roads on this cliff. The lights would appear suddenly and then fade over a period of time until you could not see them. At this time we also heard voices that sounded like radio transmissions. The voices were not understandable but they were there none the less. The same light pattern was seen by myself and Edmound Gomez as we sat on the cliff...at about 0100 hours. We also heard voices. At one time we thought we could hear trucks moving but we could not be sure about this. After 0200 hours there were no more sightings or sounds.

"On Monday, 24 October 1988 the entire party climbed to the peak once again. We were looking for evidence that there had been a crash of an 'experimental aircraft' flown by an Air Force General in 1983. This crash was reported in the newspapers for two days as a small plane and then hushed up. The craft was rumored to be a captured UFO, flown by Americans. We were hoping to prove that there indeed had been a crash but also to find some physical evidence.

"Dr. Bennewitz reported that the craft had clipped off a large tree in it's descent, had hit another tree, regained altitude, skimmed over the peak of Archuleta, [and] hit a third tree in the valley north of the peak. It was then reported to have hit the ground, flipped over twice and came to rest. We found the trees as reported by Bennewitz. They were all in line with each other and the final resting place. The first tree was about 40 inches in diameter. It was hit about 30 feet off the ground. There was no fire. I have taken samples of this tree for analysis. The other two trees were smaller [approximately 12 to 20 inches in diameter]. There was evidence of fire with these. Samples of [these] trees were also taken.

"Between the second tree and the third tree we found large pieces of what appeared to be part of the first tree. One piece was burnt while next to it was one that had not been burned. Samples were taken. While searching for physical evidence, a standard issue style ball-point pen was found. This is of the same type used by the U.S. Government but can also be purchased by the general public. It is strange to find such a pen in a remote place as this canyon. The alleged crash area showed a large SEMI-CIRCULAR area with new vegetation. The area above the semi-circular area was covered with new vegetation also.

Samples of the soil of this area were taken. Unfortunately, nothing conclusive was found when the soil was eventually analyzed.

"My overall impressions of this trip are mixed. I believe that there is definitely something going on in the area. What it is, I do not know. Perhaps there is a base there. Perhaps it is jointly operated by 'aliens' and the government, as claimed by John Lear. Then again, it could be a US base so super secret that there are no fences around to arouse any suspicion... then again I cannot say for sure. I do know that the evidence that we found and saw definitely points to the fact that something is going on in this area."

In apparent confirmation of the above, Gabe Valdez -- the former State Police officer in Dulce, New Mexico who was a part of the expedition described above, was contacted by researcher Alan deWalton in 1990, in an attempt to confirm some of the information concerning his involvement in the UFO-mutilation investigations. During a telephone conversation with Valdez, the following was learned:

"He and others HAD seen strange flying objects in the area, however he himself was unsure whether these were 'UFOs' of alien origin, or some type of top secret aircraft being tested by some secret faction of the government.

"Something DID crash near Mt. Archuleta several years ago, but again, he did not find any evidence conclusively proving whether it was an object of human OR alien origin. There is another road leading to the Mt. Archuleta area [and mesa] aside from the one which goes through the Ute Indian reservation. As for the Ute Reservation road, much of it is in good condition [paved?]. Only the area around the Archuleta region itself requires four-wheel drive vehicles.

"He did investigate cattle mutilations, and at least in SOME cases a known nerve agent was discovered in the carcasses, and other indications suggesting that the cattle were being used for research in DNA experiments."

The Dulce Wars

Chapter Three
Dulce, New Mexico and a Cosmic Conspiracy?

John Lear, a captain of a major U.S. Airline has flown over 160 different types of aircraft in over 50 different countries. He holds 17 world speed records in the Lear Jet and is the only pilot ever to hold every airman certificate issued by the Federal Aviation Administration. Mr. Lear has flown missions worldwide for the CIA and other government agencies. He has flown clandestine missions in war-zones and hot-spots around the world, often engineering hairs'-breath escapes under dangerous conditions.

A former Nevada State Senatorial candidate, he is the son of William P. Lear, designer of the Lear Jet executive airplane, the 8-track stereo, and founder of the LEAR Siegler Corporation. John Lear became interested in the subject of UFOs 13 months prior to the date given below, after talking with a friend in the United States Air Force by the name of Greg Wilson who had witnessed a UFO landing at Bentwaters AFB, near London, England, during which three small 'gray' aliens walked up to the Wing Commander.

Since then Lear has tapped his contacts in intelligence, investigating the allegations that the executive and military-industrial branches of the United States 'government' knows about, and colludes with, alien forces. Lear no longer suggests the following scenario is a 'possibility,' he emphatically states that the aliens are here, and that many of them bode us ill.

"It started after World War II," he begins. "We [the Allied forces] recovered some alien technology from Germany – not all that they had; some of it disappeared. It appears that some time in the late '30s, Germany recovered a saucer. What happened to it we don't know. But what we did get was some kind of ray gun. . ."

The following is a "Public Statement" released by John Lear on December 29, 1987 and revised on March 25, 1988. It was originally sent to some of Lear's personal friends and research associates who in turn put pressure on the Ace Pilot to release this information publicly. The first version of the statement was apparently meant for the 'inside' crowd of researchers with whom Lear associated, whereas the following revision contains the same information as the first edition, yet is directed towards the public in general:

The Dulce Wars

NOTE TO THE PRESS:

"The government of the United States continues to rely on your personal and professional gullibility to suppress the information contained herein. Your cooperation over the past 40 years has exceeded OUR wildest expectations and we salute you.

"'The sun does not revolve around the Earth. The United States Government has been in business with little gray extraterrestrials for about 20 years.

"The first truth stated here got Giordano Bruno burned at the stake in AD 1600 for daring to propose that it was real. THE SECOND TRUTH HAS GOTTEN FAR MORE PEOPLE KILLED TRYING TO STATE IT PUBLICLY THAN WILL EVER BE KNOWN. (Note: emphasis here and throughout this section is ours. - **Branton**)

"But the truth must be told. The fact that the Earth revolves around the sun was successfully suppressed by the [Roman] church for over 200 years. It eventually caused a major upheaval in the church, government, and thought. A realignment of social and traditional values. That was in the 1600's.

"Now, about 400 years after the first truth was pronounced we must again face the shocking facts. The 'horrible truth' the government has been hiding from us over 40 years. Unfortunately, the 'horrible truth' is far more horrible than the government ever imagined.

"In its effort to 'protect democracy', our government sold us to the aliens. And here is how it happened. But before I begin, I'd like to offer a word in defense of those who bargained us away. They had the best of intentions.

"Germany may have recovered a flying saucer as early as 1939. General James H. Doolittle went to Norway in 1952 to inspect a flying saucer that had crashed there in Spitzbergen.

"The 'horrible truth' was known by only a very few persons: They were indeed ugly little creatures, shaped like praying mantises. . . Of the original group that were the first to learn the 'horrible truth,' SEVERAL COMMITTED SUICIDE, the most prominent of which was Defense Secretary [and Secretary of the NAVY] James V. Forrestal who jumped to his death from a 16th story hospital window. (Note: William Cooper, a former member of a Navy Intelligence briefing team, insists that Forrestal was in fact murdered by CIA agents who made his death look like a suicide. Based on sensitive documents Cooper claims to have read, two CIA agents entered the hospital room, tied a bed sheet around Forrestal's neck and to a light fixture, and threw him out the window to hang. The bed sheet[s] broke and he fell to his death, screaming on his way down according to some witnesses "We're being invaded!" - **Branton**). Secretary Forrestal's medical records are sealed to this day.

"President Truman put a lid on the secret and turned the screws so tight that the general public still thinks that flying saucers are a joke. Have I ever got a surprise for them.

"In 1947, President Truman established a group of 12 of the top military scientific personnel of their time. They were known as MJ-12. Although the group exists today, none of the ORIGINAL members are still alive. The last one to die was Gordon Gray, former Secretary of the Army, in 1984.

"As each member passed away, the group itself appointed a new member to fill the position. There is some speculation that the group known as MJ-12 expanded to at least seven more members.

"There were several more saucer crashes in the late 1940's, one in Roswell, New Mexico; one in Aztec, New Mexico; and one near Laredo, Texas, about 30 miles inside the Mexican border.

"Consider, if you will, the position of the United States Government at that time. They proudly thought of themselves as the most powerful nation on Earth, having recently produced the atomic bomb, an achievement so stupendous, it would take Russia 4 years to catch up, and only with the help of traitors to Democracy. They had built a jet aircraft that had exceeded the speed of sound in flight. They had built jet bombers with inter-continental range that could carry weapons of enormous destruction. The post war era, and the future seemed bright.

Now imagine what it was like for those same leaders, all of whom had witnessed the panic of Orson Wells' radio broadcast, "The War of the Worlds," in 1938. Thousands of Americans panicked at a realistically presented invasion of Earth by beings from another planet. Imagine their horror as they actually viewed THE DEAD BODIES OF THESE FRIGHTENING LITTLE CREATURES WITH ENORMOUS EYES, REPTILIAN SKIN AND CLAW LIKE FINGERS.

The Dulce Wars

"Imagine their shock as they attempted to determine how these strange 'saucers' were powered and could discover no part even remotely similar to components they were familiar with: no cylinders or pistons, no vacuum tubes or turbines or hydraulic actuators. It is only when you fully understand the overwhelming helplessness the government was faced with in the late 40's that you can comprehend their perceived need for a total, thorough and sweeping cover up, to include the use of deadly force.

"The cover-up was so successful that as late as 1985 a senior scientist with the Jet Propulsion Laboratory in Pasadena, California, Dr. Al Hibbs, would look at a video tape of an enormous flying saucer and state the record, 'I'm not going to assign anything to that [UFO] phenomena without a lot more data.' Dr. Hibbs was looking at the naked emperor and saying, 'He certainly looks naked, but that doesn't prove he's naked.'

"In July 1952, a panicked government watched helplessly as a squadron of 'flying saucers' flew over Washington, D.C., and buzzed the White House, the Capitol Building, and the Pentagon. It took all the imagination and intimidation the government could muster to force that incident out of the memory of the public.

"Thousands of sightings occurred during the Korean war and several more saucers were retrieved by the Air Force. Some were stored at Wright-Patterson Air Force Base, some were stored at Air Force bases near the locations of the crash site.

"One saucer was so enormous and the logistic problems in transportation so enormous that it was buried at the crash site and remains there today. The stories are legendary on transporting crashed saucers over long distances, moving only at night, purchasing complete farms, slashing through forests, blocking major highways, sometimes driving 2 or 3 lo-boys in tandem with an extraterrestrial load a hundred feet in diameter. (It is alleged that ALPHA or BLUE Teams out of Wright-Patterson AFB were the ones who were most often mobilized to carry out "crash-retrieval" operations. - **Branton**)

"On April 30, 1964, the first communication [occurred] between these aliens and the 'U.S. Government.' (Others claim that there was an even earlier alien contact-communication in 1936 by Nazi Germany and in 1954 during the Eisenhower administration. - **Branton**)

The Dulce Wars

"During the period of 1969-1971, MJ-12 representing the U.S. Government made a deal with these creatures, called EBE's [Extraterrestrial Biological Entities, named by Detley Bronk, original MJ-12 member and 6th President of John Hopkins University]. The 'deal' was that in exchange for 'technology' that they would provide to us, we agreed to 'ignore' the abductions that were going on and suppress information on the cattle mutilations. The EBE's assured MJ-12 that the abductions [usually lasting about 2 hours] were merely the ongoing monitoring of developing civilizations.

"In fact, the purposes for the abductions turned out to be:

(1) The insertion of a 3mm spherical device through the nasal cavity of the abductee into the brain [optic and/or nerve center], the device is used for the biological monitoring, tracking, and control of the abductee.

(2) Implementation of Posthypnotic Suggestion to carry out a specific activity during a specific time period, the actuation of which will occur within the next 2 to 5 years.

(3) Termination of some people so that they could function as living sources for biological material and substances.

(4) TERMINATION OF INDIVIDUALS WHO REPRESENT A THREAT TO THE CONTINUATION OF THEIR ACTIVITY.

(5) Effect genetic engineering experiments.

(6) Impregnation of human females and early termination of pregnancies to secure the crossbreed infant.

(Note: Or perhaps a better term for it would be a "genetically altered" infant, since there has been no evidence forthcoming that an actual 'hybrid' between humans and the 'EBE' or 'Grey' species has been successful. In other words, the offspring would tend to fall to one side or the other, a 'Reptilioid' or 'Grey' entity possessing no 'soul-energy-matrix,' or a humanoid being possessing such a matrix or soul although somewhat altered genetically in it's outward physical appearance or characteristics. - **Branton**).

"The U.S. Government was NOT initially aware of the far reaching consequences of their 'deal'. They were LED to believe that the abductions were essentially benign AND SINCE THEY FIGURED THAT THE ABDUCTIONS WOULD PROBABLY GO ON ANYWAY WHETHER THEY AGREED OR NOT, they merely insisted that a current list of abductees be submitted, on a periodic basis, to MJ-12 and the National Security Council. Does this sound incredible? An actual list of abductees sent to the National Security Council? Read on, because I have news for you...

"The EBE's have a genetic disorder in that their digestive system is atrophied and not functional... In order to sustain themselves they use enzyme or hormonal secretions obtained from the tissues that they extract from humans and animals.

"The secretions obtained are then mixed with hydrogen peroxide [to kill germs, viruses, etc.] and applied on the skin by spreading or dipping parts of their bodies in the solution. The body absorbs the solution, then excretes the waste back through the skin. (Urine is also excreted through the skin in this manner, which may explain the ammonia-like STENCH that many abductees or witnesses have reported during encounters with the Grey-type 'aliens.' **Branton**).

"The cattle mutilations that were prevalent throughout the period from 1973 to 1983 and publicly noted through newspaper and magazine stories and included a documentary produced by Linda Howe for a Denver CBS affiliate KMGH-TV, were for the collection of these tissues by the aliens. The mutilations included genitals taken, rectums cored out to the colon, eyes, tongue, and throat all surgically removed with extreme precision.

"In some cases the incisions were made by cutting between the cells, a process we are not yet capable of performing in the field. In many of the mutilations there was no blood found at all in the carcass, yet there was no vascular collapse of the internal organs. THIS HAS ALSO BEEN NOTED IN THE HUMAN MUTILATIONS, one of the first of which was Sgt. Jonathan P. Lovette at the White Sands Missile Test Range in 1956, who was found three days after an Air Force Major had witnessed his abduction by a 'disk shaped' object at 0300 while on search for missile debris downrange. His genitals had been removed, rectum cored out in a surgically precise 'plug' up to the colon, eyes removed and all blood removed with, again, no vascular collapse. From some of the evidence it is apparent that this surgery is accomplished, in most cases, WHILE THE VICTIM, ANIMAL OR HUMAN, IS STILL ALIVE.

(Note: According to former Green Beret commander Bill English, THIS incident was also mentioned in the Above-Top-Secret "GRUDGE / BLUE BOOK REPORT NO. 13" which was never released with the rest of the innocuous and voluminous "Project Blue Book" reports. The "Blue Teams" who were sent on crash-retrieval operations were reportedly working on behalf of the covert branch of the Blue Book operations, and Ufological legend has it that a secret warehouse with multiple underground levels exists at Wright Patterson AFB in Ohio, one which is literally packed with alien craft, hardware, and even alien bodies 'on ice.' Wright Patterson was – and is? – the headquarters of Project Blue Book. - **Branton**)

"THE VARIOUS PARTS OF THE BODY ARE TAKEN TO VARIOUS UNDERGROUND LABORATORIES, ONE OF WHICH IS KNOWN TO BE NEAR THE SMALL NEW MEXICO TOWN OF DULCE. THIS JOINTLY OCCUPIED [CIA-ALIEN] FACILITY HAS BEEN DESCRIBED AS ENORMOUS, WITH HUGE TILED WALLS THAT 'GO ON FOREVER.' WITNESSES HAVE REPORTED HUGE VATS FILLED WITH AMBER LIQUID WITH PARTS OF HUMAN BODIES BEING STIRRED INSIDE.

"After the initial agreement, Groom Lake, one of the nations most secret test centers, was closed for a period of about a year, sometime between about 1972 and 1974, AND A HUGE UNDERGROUND FACILITY WAS CONSTRUCTED FOR AND WITH THE HELP OF THE EBE'S. THE 'BARGAINED FOR' TECHNOLOGY WAS SET IN PLACE BUT COULD ONLY BE OPERATED BY THE EBE'S THEMSELVES. NEEDLESS TO SAY, THE ADVANCED TECHNOLOGY COULD NOT BE USED AGAINST THE EBE'S THEMSELVES, EVEN IF NEEDED.

"During the period between 1979 and 1983 it became increasingly obvious to MJ-12 that things were not going as planned. IT BECAME KNOWN THAT MANY MORE PEOPLE [IN THE THOUSANDS] WERE BEING ABDUCTED THAN WERE LISTED ON THE OFFICIAL ABDUCTION

LISTS. IN ADDITION IT BECAME KNOWN THAT SOME, NOT ALL, BUT SOME OF THE NATION'S MISSING CHILDREN HAD BEEN USED FOR SECRETIONS AND OTHER PARTS REQUIRED BY THE ALIENS.

"IN 1979 THERE WAS AN ALTERCATION OF SORTS AT THE DULCE LABORATORY. A SPECIAL ARMED FORCES UNIT WAS CALLED IN TO TRY AND FREE A NUMBER OF OUR PEOPLE TRAPPED IN THE FACILITY, WHO HAD BECOME AWARE OF WHAT WAS REALLY GOING ON. ACCORDING TO ONE SOURCE 66 OF THE SOLDIERS WERE KILLED AND OUR PEOPLE WERE NOT FREED.

"By 1984, MJ-12 must have been in stark terror at the mistake they had made in dealing with the EBE's. They had subtly promoted *Close Encounters of the Third Kind* and *E.T.* to get the public used to odd looking aliens that were compassionate, benevolent and very much our 'space brothers'. MJ-12 sold the EBE's to the public, and were now faced with the fact THAT QUITE THE OPPOSITE WAS TRUE.

"In addition, a plan was formulated in 1968 to make the public aware of the existence of aliens on earth over the next 20 years to be culminated with several documentaries to be released during 1985-1987 period of time. These documentaries would explain the history and intentions of the EBE's. The discovery of the GRAND DECEPTION put the entire plans, hopes and dreams of MJ-12 into utter confusion and panic.

"Meeting at the 'Country Club,' a remote lodge with private golf course, comfortable sleeping and working quarters, and its own private airstrip built by and exclusively for the members of MJ-12, it was a factional fight of what to do now. PART OF MJ-12 WANTED TO CONFESS THE WHOLE SCHEME AND SHAMBLES IT HAD BECOME TO THE PUBLIC, BEG THEIR FORGIVENESS AND ASK FOR THEIR SUPPORT.

The other part [the majority] of MJ-12 argued that there was no way they could do that, that the situation was untenable and there was no use in exciting the public with the 'horrible truth' and that the best plan was to continue the development of a weapon that could be used against the EBE's under the guise of SDI, the Strategic Defense Initiative (Star Wars), which had nothing whatsoever to do with a defense for inbound Russian nuclear missiles. As these words are being written, Dr. Edward Teller, 'father' of the H-Bomb is personally in the test tunnels of the Nevada Test Site, driving his workers and associates in the words of one, 'like a man possessed.' And well he should, for Dr. Teller is a member of MJ-12 along with Dr. Kissinger, Admiral Bobby Inman, and possibly Admiral Poindexter, to name a few of the current members of MJ-12.

"Before the 'Grand Deception' was discovered and according to a meticulous plan for metered release of information to the public, several documentaries and video tapes were made.

"William Moore, a Burbank, California, based UFO researcher who wrote *The Roswell Incident* – a book published in 1980 that detailed the crash, recovery and subsequent cover-up of a UFO with 4 alien bodies – has a video tape of 2 newsmen interviewing a military officer associated with MJ-12. This military officer answers questions relating to the history of MJ-12 and the cover-up, the recovery of a number of flying saucers and the existence of a live alien [one of three living aliens captured and designated, or named, EBE-1, EBE-2, and EBE-3, being held in a facility designated as YY-II at Los Alamos, New Mexico.

"The only other facility of this type, which is electromagnetically secure, is at Edwards Air Force Base in Mojave, California. The officer names as previously mentioned plus a few others: Harold Brown, Richard Helms, Gen. Vernon Walters, JPL's Dr. Allen and Dr. Theodore van Karman, to name a few of the current and past members of MJ-12.

"The officer also relates the fact that the EBE's claim to have created Christ. The EBE's have a type of recording device that has recorded all of Earth's history and can display it in the form of a hologram. This hologram can be filmed but because of the way holograms work does not come out very clear on movie film or video tape. The crucifixion of Christ on the Mount of Olives (this actually took place on the hill Calvary, not the Mt. of Olives - **Branton**) has allegedly been put on film to show the public. The EBE's 'claim' to have created Christ, which, IN VIEW OF THE GRAND DECEPTION, COULD BE AN EFFORT TO DISRUPT TRADITIONAL VALUES FOR UNDETERMINED REASONS.

"Another video tape allegedly in existence is an interview with an EBE. Since EBE's communicate telepathically (via psionic crystalline transceiver-like implants that link the Greys together into a mass collective-hive-mind - **Branton**), an Air Force Colonel serves as interpreter. Just before the recent stock market correction in October of 1987, several newsmen, including Bill Moore, had been invited to Washington D.C., to personally film the EBE in a similar type interview, and distribute the film to the public. Apparently, because of the correction in the market, it was felt the timing was not propitious. In any case, it certainly seems like an odd method to inform the public of extraterrestrials, but it would be in keeping with the actions of A PANICKED ORGANIZATION WHO AT THIS POINT IN TIME DOESN'T KNOW WHICH WAY TO TURN.

"Moore is also in possession of more Aquarius documents, a few pages of which leaked out several years ago and detailed the supersecret NSA project which had been denied by them until just recently. In a letter to Senator John Glenn, NSA's Director of Policy, Julia B. Wetzel, wrote, 'Apparently there is or was an Air Force project with the name [Aquarius] which dealt with UFO's.

Coincidentally, there is also an NSA project by that name.' NSA's project AQUARIUS deals specifically with 'communications with the aliens' [EBE's]. Within the Aquarius program was project 'Snowbird,' a project to test-fly a recovered alien aircraft at Groom Lake, Nevada. This project continues today at that location. In the words of an individual who works at Groom Lake, 'Our people are much better at taking things apart than they are at putting them back together.'

"Moore, who claims he has a contact with MJ-12, feels that they have been stringing him along, slipping him documents and providing him with leads, promising to go public with some of the information on extraterrestrials by the end of 1987.

"Certain of Moore's statements lead one to believe that Moore himself is a government agent working for MJ-12, not to be strung alone, but to string along ever hopeful UFOlogists that the truth is just around the corner. Consider.

> (1) Moore states emphatically that he is not a government agent, although when Lee Graham [a Southern California based UFOlogist] was investigated by DIS [Defense Investigative Service] for possession of classified documents received from Moore, Moore himself was not.

(2) Moore states emphatically that the cattle mutilations of 1973-1983 were a hoax by Linda Howe [producer of *A Strange Harvest*] to create publicity for herself. He cites the book *Mute Evidence* as the bottom line of the hoax. *Mute Evidence* was a government sponsored book to explain the mutilations in conventional terms.

(3)Moore states that the U.S.A.F. Academy physics book, *Introductory Space Science*, vol. II chapter 13, entitled 'Unidentified Flying Objects', which describes four of the most commonly seen aliens [one of which is the EBE] was written by Lt. Col. Edward R. Therkelson and Major Donald B. Carpenter, Air Force personnel who did not know what they were talking about and were merely citing 'crackpot' references. He, Moore, states that the book was withdrawn to excise the chapter.

"If the government felt they were being forced to acknowledge the existence of aliens on Earth because of the overwhelming evidence such as the October and November sightings in Wytheville, Va., and recently released books such as *Night Siege* [Hynek, J. Allen; Imbrogno, Phillip J.; Pratt, Bob: Ballantine Books, Random House, New York], and taking into consideration the Grand Deception AND OBVIOUSLY HOSTILE INTENT OF THE EBE'S, it might be expedient for MJ-12 to admit the EBE's but conceal the information on the mutilations and abductions.

"If MJ-12 and Moore were in some kind of agreement then it would be beneficial to Moore to tow the party line. For example, MJ-12 would say... 'here are some more genuine documents... but remember... no talking about the mutilations or abductions.' This would be beneficial to Moore as it would supply the evidence to support his theory that E.T.s exist but deny the truths about the E.T.s. However, if Moore was indeed working for MJ-12, he would follow the party line anyway. . . admitting the E.T.s but pooh poohing the mutilations and abductions. If working alone, Moore might not even be aware of the Grand Deception. The controversy continues today with Moore claiming he had no involvement with MJ-12 or the probable hoax of the alleged *MJ-12 Papers*.

The Dulce Wars

"Time will tell. It is possible that Moore will go ahead and release the video interview with the military officer around the first of the year, as he has promised. From MJ-12's point of view, the public would be exposed to the information without really having to believe it because Moore is essentially not as credible a source as, say, the President of the United States. After a few months of digestion and discussion, a more credible source could emerge with a statement that yes in fact the interview was essentially factual.

"Now you ask, 'Why haven't I heard any of this?' Who do you think you would hear it from? Dan Rather? Tom Brokaw? Sam Donaldson? Wrong. These people just read the news, they don't find it. They have ladies who call and interview witnesses and verify statements on stories coming over the wire [either **AP** or **UPI**].

"It's not like Dan Rather would go down to Wytheville, Virginia, and dig into why there were FOUR THOUSAND reported sightings in October and November of 1987. Better Tom Brokaw or someone else should risk their credibility on this type of story. Tom Brokaw? Tom wants Sam Donaldson to risk his credibility. No one, but no one, is going to risk their neck on such outlandish ideas, regardless of how many people report sightings of 900 foot objects running them off the road. In the case of the Wytheville sightings, dozens of vans with NASA lettered on the side failed to interest newsmen. And those that asked questions were informed that NASA was doing a weather survey.

"Well then, you ask, what about our scientists? Wouldn't they have known? If Carl Sagan knew, then he was committing a great fraud through the solicitation of memberships in the Planetary Society, 'to search for extraterrestrial intelligence'. Another charade into which the U.S. Government dumps millions of dollars every year is the radio-telescope in Arecibo, Puerto Rico, operated by Cornell University. Cornell is ostensibly searching for signals from Outer Space, a sign maybe, that somebody is out there. It is hard to believe that relatively intelligent astronomers could be so ignorant. Actually, it is not ignorance, but fear of disturbing the scientific 'status quo.'

(Note: Also, even if they did find evidence of extraterrestrial life, do you think that SETI and similar government-sponsored projects would tell US about It? Let's just take a look at some actual statements from those involved with these projects. The following is a quote from Matt Spetalnick's article "IS

ANYBODY OUT THERE? NASA LOOKS FOR REAL ET'S", in *REUTERS* Magazine, Oct. 5, 1992: "At least 70 times scientists have picked up radio waves that bore the marks of communication by beings from other worlds, but they were never verified, Frank Drake said." And researcher John Spencer, in a reference to Dr. Otto Strove, tells how this astrophysicist assisted Frank Drake in establishing Project OZMA, and it's very mysterious conclusion: "...the project began its search by focusing on the star TAU CETI. According to claims made at the time, AS SOON AS the project got underway STRONG INTELLIGENT SIGNALS were picked up, leaving all the scientists stunned. Abruptly, Dr. Strove then declared Project OZMA had been shut down, and commented that there was no sensible purpose for listening to messages from another world." [*THE UFO ENCYCLOPEDIA*].

"So then, these 'insiders' will accept ALL of our hard-earned tax dollars to finance their radio projects -- if not their underground bases and covert space operations. Yet cursed be any 'mere mortal' for having the audacity to actually insist on having access to the products of their 'financial investments'! - **Branton**)

"If the government won't tell us the truth and the major networks won't even give it serious consideration (Note: This was written before such programs as SIGHTINGS, ENCOUNTERS, UNSOLVED MYSTERIES, CURRENT AFFAIR, MONTEL WILLIAMS, STRANGE UNIVERSE and other TV news digests and talk shows DID begin dealing with the UFO phenomena, abductions, and so on in much greater depth – not to mention the X-FILES, DARK SKIES and other TV series'. - **Branton**), then what is the big picture, anyway? Are the EBE's, having done a hundred thousand or more abductions [possibly millions worldwide], built AN UNTOLD NUMBER OF SECRET UNDERGROUND BASES [Groom Lake, Nevada; Sunspot, Datil, Roswell, and Pie Town, New Mexico, just to name a few] getting ready to return to wherever they came from? Or, from the obvious preparations are we to assume that they are getting ready for a big move? or is [it] the more sinister and most probable situation that the invasion is essentially complete and it is all over but the screaming?

"A well planned invasion of Earth for it's resources and benefits would not begin with mass landings or ray-gun equipped aliens. A properly planned and executed invasion by a civilization thousands [of] years in advance of us would most likely be complete before a handful of people, say 12?, realized what was happening. No fuss, no mess. The best advice I can give you is this: Next time you see a flying saucer and are awed by its obvious display of technology and gorgeous lights of pure color - RUN LIKE HELL!"

June 3, 1988 Las Vegas, NV

[The following was an addendum to the above that was included with later copies of John Lear's 'statement']:

"In 1983 when the Grand Deception was discovered MJ-12 [which may now be designated 'PI-40'] started work on a weapon or some kind of device to contain the EBE's which had by now totally infested our society. This program was funded through SDI which, coincidentally, was initiated at approximately the same date. A frantic effort has been made over the past 4 years by all participants. This program ended in failure in December of 1987.

(Note: British Ufologist Timothy Good claimed that over 22 British scientists, who were working on the U.S. SDI program for British Marconi and other Aerospace companies -- had all mysteriously died or 'committed suicide' within the space of a few years. Could this have had anything to do with this 'failure'? Apparently someone 'out there' was intent on sabotaging the SDI / STAR WARS project. Also there are reports that several of our 'defense satellites' have been mysteriously destroyed as well. - **Branton**).

"A new program has been conceived but will take about 2 years to develop. In the meantime, it is absolutely essential to MJ-12 [PI-40], that no one, including the Senate, the Congress or the Citizens of the United States of America [or anyone else for that matter] become aware of the real circumstances surrounding the UFO cover-up and total disaster it has become.

"Moore never did release the video tapes but claims he is negotiating with a major network to do so. . .soon."

Another source added the following statements in regards to Lear's claims: "Area 51... and a similar setup near Dulce, New Mexico, may now belong to forces not loyal to the U.S. Government, or even the human race. 'It's horrifying to think that all the scientists we think are working for us [in the joint-interaction bases] are actually controlled by aliens.'

"'. . .SDI, regardless of what you hear, was completed. . .to shoot down incoming saucers. The mistake was that we thought they were coming inbound, in fact, they're already here. They're in underground bases all over the place.' It seems that the aliens had constructed many such bases without our knowledge, where they conduct heinous genetic experiments on animals, human beings, and 'improvised' creatures of their own making.

"Thus was born PROJECT EXCALIBUR. Press reports described EXCALIBUR as a weapons system designed to obliterate deeply-buried Soviet command centers, which the Reagan administration hypocritically characterized as destabilizing. We have exactly similar centers. Lear claims the weapon was actually directed toward the internal alien threat. Unfortunately, the 'visitors' have invaded us in more ways than one.

"'Millions of Americans have been implanted. There's a little device that varies in size from 50 microns to 3 millimeters; it is inserted through the nose into the brain. It effectively controls the person. Dr. [J. Allen] Hynek estimated in 1972 that one in every 40 Americans was implanted; we believe it may be as high as one in ten now.' These implants will be activated at some time in the near future, for some unspecified alien purpose. It is believed that many 'implantees' are being mentally controlled with specific tasks to be enacted at a later date.'"

When Lear was pressed to disclose some of his sources, he stated that his anonymous intelligence informants "go right to the top." He did however mention some of the names in not-so-sensitive intelligence positions from whom he has also gathered information, many of these names may be familiar to veteran Ufologists. These include:

Paul Bennewitz, director of Thunder Scientific Laboratories [a New Mexico-based research facility with government contract ties], who claims to have gained access to and 'interrogated' an alien computer system via a radio-video-computer setup of his own invention.

Linda Howe, the television documentarian responsible for *STRANGE HARVEST* [a program about cattle mutilations], who received astonishing 'leaks' from a special intelligence officer, Colonel Richard Doty formerly of Kirtland AFB, a name noted in aerial research circles. It should be considered that Doty may be responsible for spreading UFO disinformation.

The Dulce Wars

Robert Collins [code-named 'Condor', according to Lear], who has secured numerous official documents relating to UFOs.

Sgt. Clifford Stone, premiere collector of UFO related Freedom of Information Act or FOIA documents.

As an interesting follow-up to Lear's article, I will quote some actual statements made by prominent individuals in regards to the 'UFO' phenomenon:

"In our obsession with antagonisms of the moment, we often forget how much unites all the members of humanity. Perhaps we need some outside, universal threat to make us realize this common bond. I occasionally think how quickly our differences would vanish if we were facing an alien threat from outside this world. And yet, I ask you, IS NOT AN ALIEN FORCE ALREADY AMONG US?"

President Ronald Reagan., Remarks made to the 42nd General Assembly of the United Nations., Sept. 21, 1987

"I couldn't help but say to him [Gorbachev], just think how easy his task and mine might be in these meetings that we held if suddenly there was a threat to this world from some other species from another planet outside in the universe... Well, I don't suppose we can wait for some alien race to come down and threaten us. But I think that between us we can bring about that realization."

President Ronald Reagan., Remarks to Fallston High School students and Faculty, Fallston, MD., October 4, 1985

"For your confidential information, a reliable and confidential source has advised the Bureau that flying disks are believed to be man-made missiles rather than natural phenomenon. It has also been determined that for approximately the past four years the USSR has been engaged in experimentation on an unknown type of flying disk."

FBI Memo, dated March 25, 1949 sent to a large number of FBI offices.

"...on Unidentified Flying Objects... The panel recommends that the national security agencies institute policies... designed to prepare the material defenses and the morale of the country to recognize... and react most effectively to true indications of hostile measures."

Recommendation of the CIA Robertson Panel on UFOs., January, 1953

"Public interest in disclosure is far outweighed by the sensitive nature of the materials and the obvious effect on national security their release may entail."

U.S. District Court Opinion in the case of Citizens Against UFO Secrecy vs. the National Security Agency., May 18, 1982

"The sums made available to the Agency may be expended without regard to the provisions of law and regulations relating to the expenditures of Government."

Central Intelligence Act of 1949

"On this land a flying disk has been found intact, with eighteen three-foot tall human-LIKE occupants, all dead in it but not burned."

FBI memo from New Orleans Branch to Director, FBI, March 31, 1950 about a disk found in the Mojave desert in January, 1950

"When four sit down to conspire, three are fools and the fourth is a government agent."

Duncan Lunan.

"The flying disks are real."

General Nathan Twining.

Ace Pilot John Lear has some fantastic things to say about UFOs. Photo by Ed Biebel

Chapter Four
Dulce New Mexico & the Nazi Connection

Researcher Jim Bennett, in a letter to Jacques Vallee dated Jan. 15, 1992, made some startling disclosures in regards to the alien situation and the Dulce, N.M. base in particular. It is my belief that even if there is a fascist-CIA cabal trying to establish a world dictatorship using the 'threat' of an alien invasion to foment world government, that the 'threat' may be real all the same.

It is also possible that the 'Bavarians' may be working with very REAL aliens in an end-game designed to establish a world government using this 'threat' as an excuse to do so, although when the world is under 'their' control the Illuminati may betray the human race by turning much of the global government control-system over to the Grey aliens [the Beast?].

The aliens may have been collaborating with the Bavarians for a very long time as part of their agenda to implement absolute electronic control over the inhabitants of planet earth.

One source, an Area 51 worker – and member of a secret Naval Intelligence group called COM-12 – by the name of Michael Younger, stated that the Bavarian Black Nobility [secret societies] have agreed to turn over three-quarters of the planet to the Greys if they could retain 25 percent for themselves and have access to alien mind-control technology.

The aliens would assist in the abduction, programming and implanting of people throughout the world in preparation for a New World Order – which in turn would be annexed to the alien empire.

Apparently some top-echelon Bavarians have agreed to this, since they realize that they NEED the alien mind-control and implant technology in order to carry out their plans for world domination. In his lengthy letter, Jim Bennett, director of the research organization 'PLANET-COM', writes:

"...1947 brought the passage of the National Security Act, the start of the NAZI GERMINATED CIA and NSA. The influx of at least a hundred Nazi scientists, engineers, etc., into the United States and Canada. (Note: Other sources claim that eventually over 3000 Nazi S.S. agents entered the U.S. in this manner. NOT former Nazis but ACTIVE Nazi SS who still maintained the national socialist philosophy and agendas which they intended to carry through on to their planned conclusion. They were given refuge within the military-industrial complex with the help of members of the Bavarian-based black gnostic, serpent worshiping lodges in America, such as the Jesuit-spawned Scottish Rite and related lodges who control the oil-military-industrial complex. The leaders of the Military-Industrial Complex or M.I.C. not only gave these fascists refuge following the war, but also had financed the Nazi war machine itself during the second world war. - **Branton**).

"A Nazi aeronautical engineer, a certain Herr Mieth – who had designed four different types of saucer shaped craft by 1943 using either rocket power or DONUT CONFIGURATION jet turbine engines, with the cabin stabilized by gyro, the compressors rotating in one direction and the expansion chambers and vectored exhausts rotating in the opposite direction – was traced to Canada in 1947 and began work for the A. V. Roe company [Avro disk]. The phony AVRO Aircar was definitely to disinform the press as to the real projects underway underground in Canada.

"The eight mile long train that went out of Austria in 1945 [672 train cars!], to the coast of Brittany, the contents loaded on board SHIPS, eventually end[ed] up underground in Southwestern Canada. At the same time over 100 prefab factory buildings were shipped from England to British Columbia.

"...the Nazis had everything before any other country, they had radar in 1933, they had infra-red sensors, heavy water, etc., etc. We have been told lie after lie in terms of who invented these things. If anyone in the world had access to 'alien' technology it was the. . .'Aryans' [Nazis]. Their metallurgy and casting were flawed or they would have conquered the world. As you probably know, many expatriate Nazis were given carte blanche, new I.D.'s., and were included in [the] startup of more than several departments of the CIA in 1947. Departments including genetics and cloning [with some of the same doctors who had given death camp residents gangrene, etc.], designer drugs and mind control using the same scientists who had designed Methadone and Methedrine for Hitler's maniac efforts. In 1952, a public stir caused the CIA to shuffle these fab fellows out of town. My guess is to various underground centers that were being built.

"...I have talked to Paul Bennewitz at length, several times. On his behalf, you only tell people how they drove him nuts, not why. I ask myself why would you leave out that reason why they sent him reeling? (here Bennett is addressing

The Dulce Wars

Jacques Vallee concerning his book ***REVELATIONS* - Branton**). To fill you in, because you obviously took Linda Howe's and Tracy's opinion rather than questioning Paul directly; he's a pilot, he flew over the Dulce area numerous times on his way between Albuquerque and Denver. He took many pictures of the construction going on, and according to Paul, he also took pictures of circular craft on the ground at this site which, as late as 1973 according to him, had large hanger doors much the same as Lazar's second hand explanation about the doors at S-4. [All the stuff from Area 51 and 'S-4' having to do with inertial mass cancellation was moved to an area NEAR ST. GEORGE, UTAH].

"The most revealing photos and their negatives disappeared in about 1975 when various 'fringe UFO experts' visited Paul. Also, his house was burglarized and ransacked more than once. In later years Moore, Shandera, and Torme made a meaningless tour of Dulce when they went on to Albuquerque [the real reason for their travels] to see if there was any more evidence of serious consequence still in Paul's possession that they could grab, and sure enough, he was missing some photos when they left his house. If you even talked to Bennewitz, you would have gotten a lot closer to having a 'revelation'. . .

"The 'waste' from the underground bio-genetic lab [no aliens involved, although that is where we humans produce the short lived, big-eyed, big headed imitation aliens] comes out in the river canyon about TEN MILES BELOW Navajo Dam...(Note: An alternative scenario to the above would be that reptoid grey aliens ARE involved – AS WELL AS biogenetically constructed beings developed by Illuminati-Thule-CIA backed scientists working in the Dulce facility - **Branton**)

"Although these days they 'treat' it a lot more before letting their 'grey' water back into the environment. This base and others are of course connected by tunnels to Los Alamos. The Archuleta Mesa installation rivals Pine Gap at Alice Springs, Australia for security, etc. Every U.S. Air Force base has a so-called 'bolt-hole' and is connected to this bolt-hole by tunnel...

"A group of 21 people led by an individual we will call Rick, went to Area 51 in 1989 in a small bus to watch 'saucers'. They were stopped on 'mail-box road' by two individuals carrying automatic weapons and wearing camouflage togs. One individual popped a can of 'gas' in the aisle of the bus, and that's all for three hours. When they came to their senses, they cut their trip short, returned to L.A.

and five persons got separately regressed using hypnotic regressors that did not know one another, and found that during the lost time their memories had repressed similar events. They had been marched off the bus, taken in jeeps to a building nearby, and had their lives threatened by military personnel...

"In the U.S., the group that runs the 'alien abduction scam' can only use some of the hardiest of these short lived bio-genetic bad luck stories. Short lived because they have no digestive tract and can survive only about two weeks maximum after they are removed from the growing matrix, then they deteriorate and die. They have no soul and are not considered 'sentient beings' by Tibetan Buddhists."

(Note: One might ask, why would they bother? The REPTILIAN Greys, the cloned branch – although in addition to the clones there are also apparently the polyembryons and egg-layers – reportedly have no digestive tract and thus intake food and excrete waste through the skin. Jim Bennett may have just assumed that, since they have no digestive tract they had no way of taking-in food, and that they were therefore government creations which die after two weeks of starving. We grant however that Bennett is right in that – according to the **DULCE PAPERS** – human and cattle DNA may be used to develop "Almost Humans", and other unnatural living forms - **Branton**)

"...The army's mind control unit must take well deserved credit for the veterans who seemingly go suddenly crazy, killing many people and then themselves. The most recent event in Killeen, Texas was planned for the day BEFORE a Congressional vote on gun control, hoping to influence Congress with yet another mass automatic killing. Handlers [psychiatrists] at each perpetrators's local Veterans Hospital are involved in each and every case of these mass killings/suicides. Prozac is also involved with each case having been prescribed by the aforementioned 'handlers' in each and every case. The fellow in Canada who killed 12 women at a women's college, the fellow in Stockton, California schoolyard, etc. etc...."

Sirhan Sirhan, the man who was convicted of murdering Senator Robert Kennedy, had a psychiatrist by the name of Dr. Diamond who maintained CIA-fascist connections. Also Sirhan's attorney Grant Cooper, who seemingly made very little effort to defend Sirhan, had CIA-fascist ties as well, leading some to believe that Sirhan was used as a hypno-programmed "Manchurian

Candidate" by a fascist cabal, a cabal that murdered not only Robert Kennedy but also his brother President John F. Kennedy as well. Following World War II over 2,000 German immigrants to the U.S. became members of the American Psychiatric Association, which was involved in GUN CONTROL lobbying. In light of the collaboration between the Bavarian Thule Society and the Bavarian Illuminati, and the influx of Thule-backed fifth-column Nazi SS agents into U.S. Intelligence, with the help of Illuminati-backed Oil barons like the German-immigrant Aryan-supremacist Rockefellers and their corporate oil-chemical empires [EXXON, ARCO, ZAPATA, etc.], and in light of the deadly intent of both 'Bavarian' societies to establish a "New World Order" as Adolph Hitler laid out in his second book "The New World Order," one has to wonder WHY so many German nationals would join an association that dealt directly with the study of people's MINDS?

This is not to say that Germans themselves are to blame, it is rather the German-Bavarian FASCISTS who are behind the New World Order agenda, and especially the Satanist Germanic Black Nobility families who claim direct descent from the early leaders of the [un]Holy Roman Empire of Germany, which rose from the remnant of the Roman Empire and which kept Europe in an iron grip throughout the Dark Ages. These were the "13 families" who had ruled vast financial empires in Europe for nearly 1500 years. They are once again trying to take control of the world as they attempted to do with World Wars I and II, provoke a global war that will result in the massive 'de-population' of Blacks, Asians, Jews, Slavs, and many others – excepting of course for the 'Aryan elite' class. In essence they intend to finish what Adolph Hitler set out to accomplish. The threat then is from 'Nazism' or National 'Socialism', whether it be European, British or American or whether it be political, corporate or occult National Socialism.

Some have reported that the sudden 'fall' of the Soviet states and the Berlin wall was planned in advance as part of an agenda to merge the East and the West into a so called communist-socialist/democratic-socialist New World Order. East and West Berlin would be at the forefront for the reunification of Eastern and Western Europe and in turn – they hope – the rest of the world. Germany has also led the way for European unification by establishing an 'open border' policy and encouraging other European countries to do the same. This may sound   benign on the outside but considering the facts it may be a ruse to unify Europe under German control, which was also Adolph Hitler's goal. However in this case the unification is being accomplished through economic means rather than military means.

The control is still in Germany but it is more subtle. The Third Reich established German MILITARY control of Europe. The European Economic Community or E.E.C. established ECONOMIC control. In most cases, in this world it is the ECONOMIC forces which control governments. Sad, but true. Notice how the term "Economic" has now been removed, and the New World Order has been re-named the European Community. Very clever! In other words the unification is no longer just along economic lines but is becoming increasingly political, since the member nations have been pressured into submitting to an E.C. constitution along MORE THAN mere economic lines.

France and England have been pulled into this alliance, in spite of two devastating world wars with the very country that is secretly orchestrating the E.C. or the New World Order. Come on France and England, wake up!

Germany is not only the largest federated state in the E.C., but in 1990 was the LARGEST economic power in the WORLD, with a trade surplus totaling over $58 billion. With almost no foreign currency reserves in 1949, Germany had accumulated nearly $80 billion in reserves by 1989, compared with the $38 billion in the U.S.A. and $41 billion in Great Britain. A rather incredible comeback for a country that had waged two world wars for the sole purpose of offensive conquest, wars that had cost the Allies a HEAVY price in blood and resources.

Of course Germany is also the LEADING economic power in the E.C. as well, possessing 35% of the Economic power-base of the European Community according to the GROLIER ENCYCLOPEDIA. So just WHERE does the real power lie in the E.C. / N.W.O? Considering that the German Black Nobility were the same ones who sent Vladimir Lenin from GERMANY to Russia to start the Communist Revolution, AND the same powers who backed Adolph Hitler... then it is not surprising that Communist East Germany would merge into Democratic(?) West Germany with such ease.

It should not be surprising, therefore, to learn that GERMAN troops in the United States AND Canada play a MAJOR role in the planned invasion of North

America under the cover of a United Nations emergency action. Lenin himself revealed the ultimate goal of the Communist agenda, on behalf of the Bavarian elite whom he served. Communism, like Democracy, was supposed to give control of the government to the PEOPLE. But of course Lenin altered the plan a little bit – just as the largely unelected-appointed Executive branch of the American government altered the rules of democracy – and stated that he did not believe that the common people could handle the responsibility of directing the Communist Revolution, so a select group of individuals trained in the Communist philosophy would carry out this responsibility instead. And wouldn't you know it, many of these people who ended up as the leaders of the Communist Revolution were hand-picked by the German-immigrant Capitalist Rockefeller family themselves. "Oh what a tangled web we weave." The Bavarian cultists who were REALLY running the show would of course be the "WE" that Lenin refers to in the following quote:

"First WE will TAKE Russia, next WE will CAPTURE the nations of eastern Europe, then WE will TAKE the masses of Asia. Finally, WE will SURROUND the United States and that last bastion of freedom will fall into our hands like over-ripe fruit."

A likely scenario that some have suggested would be an orchestrated global economic collapse – blamed on Americans of course – which would be followed by fomented anarchy in American cities, followed by sudden nuclear strikes on strategic military bases on the East and West coasts, followed by a Chinese invasion of the West coast, a Russian invasion via Alaska, and a United Nations / German invasion via the East and North-East coasts of the U.S.A.

Collaborating with a Bavarian-backed United Nations - New World Order agenda can only lead to the DEATH of your independence as a nation, the DEATH of your culture and history, and the DEATH of your children who are sent to fight and die for the sake of a Global Government, its Bavarian-Antarctican masters, and in turn their 'Draconian' allies who are just waiting with greedy claws to take hold of this planet once they have succeeded in getting us to kill each other off to the point where they can move right in and take over with little human resistance.

For further information, be sure to read: ***Evil Agenda of the Secret Government*** by Tim Swartz, and published by Global Communications.

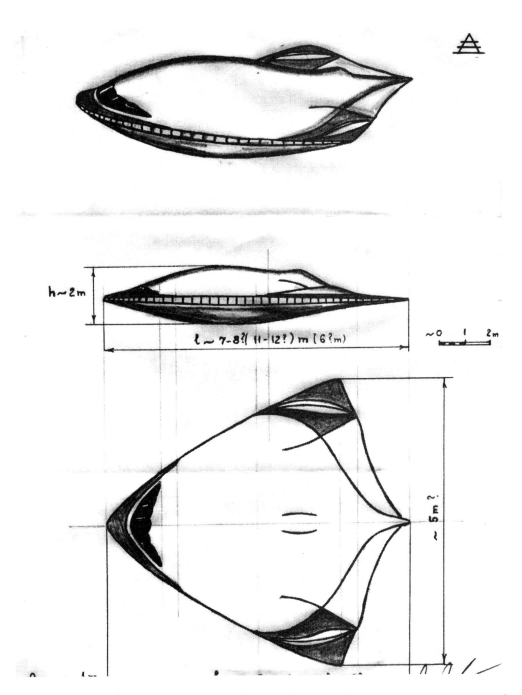

Nazi Germany is believed to have recovered
a Crashed UFO in 1936. German scientists
developed their own crude versions near
the end of the war. Drawing by Anton Anfalow

Chapter Five
Report from a Japanese Television Crew

Norio Hayakawa is the head of the 'CIVILIAN INTELLIGENCE NETWORK' [P.O. Box 599., Gardena, CA 80248]. Mr. Hayakawa was one of several individuals, including a Japanese film crew from the NIPPON Television Network in Japan, who witnessed and video-taped "a flight maneuver of a brightly lit orange-yellowish light making extremely unorthodox flight patterns, including sudden acceleration, descension and ascension – possibly exerting a force of multiple g's under extremely limited space and time – and even zig-zag type movements, while on a field trip to an area just outside of 'Area 51' in Nevada on Wednesday, February 21, 1990" [there were approximately 25 to 28 individuals in the group who also witnessed the display]. His brother-in-law Itsuro Isokawa also photographed the object as it was in flight.

With over 30 years of in-depth UFO investigative experience, Norio was instrumental in the subsequent production of a two-hour documentary program televised throughout Japan on March 24, 1990. The entire program dealt with Area 51 and also the crew's pursuit of an alleged biogenetics laboratory in New Mexico, that is, the DULCE facility. It is his contention that what could only be described as "...highly intelligent and deceptive 'ultradimensional entities' materializing in disguise as aliens, are collaborating with a secret world government that is preparing (barring unexpected circumstances - **Branton**) to ingeniously stage a contact-landing...to bring about a New World Order."

(Note: This Alien-Bavarian collaboration is apparently feigning animosity with one another by pushing for global government so that the world can join together to "fight the aliens." As in Vietnam and Korea where the Socialist leaders of the United Nations Organization were playing both sides of the chessboard, any war waged by the New World Order against the Greys will no doubt be a no-win conflict that will only serve to reduce the population of the planet, which is after all part and parcel of the overall Draconian-Bavarian global agenda.

Another possibility that has been suggested is that the Greys will be made out to be the good guys who need our help to break free from the tall Reptoids and their empire, which had conquered them in the past, or visa versa. Actually the collaboration between the Reptoids and Greys has been undertaken with the full consent of both sides, and behind the scenes the collectivist Reptoids, the Insectoids, the Greys and the Bavarian secret society lodges are all working together. Many scenarios are possible. . . however the important thing to remember is that ANY war waged against the Reptilian Greys which threatens the American Declaration of Independence, the U.S. Constitution and the Bill of Rights is merely playing into the hands of the aliens either way you look at it. International cooperation in a common defense against an alien threat should be considered SO LONG AS the national sovereignty of individual nations are not violated in the process.

All nations should learn to be self-supporting and not be tempted to succumb to a global economic system – and therefore a global political system, in that money and politics are more or less synonymous... at least in this world where those who control the money CONTROL the governments. Also independent economies will prevent all nations from falling like dominoes if an economic collapse does occur.

The target of any future attacks against an outside threat to a nation's security should not be exclusive ONLY to the aliens NOR exclusively against human conspirators or tyrants, but the target of any future conflict with one or the other – in regards to planetary or national defense – should be directed specifically at those areas where collaboration and interaction between the alien infiltrators AND the human collaborators are taking place. . . for instance areas such as the underground 'joint-interaction' bases of Neuschwabenland, Antarctica; Pine Gap, Australia; Alsace-Lorraine Mts. area of France-Germany; and of course and probably by far the worst of all, the underground mega-complex below DULCE, NEW MEXICO where the worst life-forms this universe has to offer seemingly congregate, conceive and carry out their atrocities against their victims – or those who have been taken or abducted to the base permanently – as well as against their implanted-programmed victims beyond the confines of the base who are never-the-less forced to exist in psychological concentration camps imposed on them against their will by the collaboration. - **Branton**)

Furthermore, Norio Hayakawa contends that the GRAND DECEPTION will immediately follow a rapid series of shocking, incredible events in succession, beginning with a Russia-backed Arab Confederacy's attempt to invade Israel, simultaneous worldwide earthquakes, worldwide stock market crash and a sudden, mysterious evacuation of a segment of the planet's population, all of which will culminate in a quick official formation of a New World Order [based in Europe] that will last for seven years upon its inception.

(Note: It is interesting that George Washington's famous 'vision' at Valley Forge accurately predicted the Revolutionary and Civil wars and their outcome, and also a 'third trial' through which America must pass. . .an air, ground and sea invasion of the America's by a World Order which will have conquered all of Asia, Africa and Europe. Depending on how one interprets the prophecies of Revelation, this siege will last for either 3 ½ or 7 years, and will end with an American victory aided by Divine Intervention.

I personally believe that America is the 'wilderness' spoken of in the 12th chapter of the book of Revelation. Since the world empire will last no longer than 7 years according to the books of DANIEL and REVELATION, the invasion/siege of America must also not exceed 7 years, although I suspect that it will be closer to 3 ½ years.

Also Washington's vision combined with other prophetic sources seem to imply that those who are living west of the Mississippi river at this time will be far better off then those in the 'occupied' zone east of the Mississippi. If General Washington's vision was accurate, then the ultimate outcome of the battle is not the question. The real question is how many Americans, North-Central-South Americans, will survive through to the final victory? - **Branton**)

Norio also explains that the Grand Deception and the shocking series of events will: "...put millions and millions of people worldwide in an absolute stupor for months during which time a special, extremely effective, multi-leveled 'mind control' program will be activated to calm down the stunned populace."

Hayakawa has himself appeared on Japanese television, has lectured considerably, has appeared on a radio station in Phoenix, Arizona, and has been the subject of an article in the *ARIZONA REPUBLIC*, has published articles in *U.S. Japanese Business News* [March, 1990], was the guest on a Japanese talk show in March and April of 1990, and also appeared on the Billy Goodman *Happening* on KVEG of Las Vegas several times in early 1990, and in 1995 made dramatic appearances on Art Bell's *DREAMLAND* broadcast. He was also interviewed on the Anthony J. Hilder Show on *Radio Free America* aired in Anchorage, Alaska, during all of which he spoke extensively about his interesting beliefs concerning the origin and nature of UFO's. In a letter dated January 28, 1991, Norio added the following comments concerning the Dulce facility and it's possible connection with the 'Mystery of Iniquity' of Bible prophecy: "I've been to Dulce with the Nippon Television Network crew and interviewed many, many people over there and came back with the firm conviction that something was happening around 10 to 15 years ago over there, including nightly sightings of strange lights and appearances of military jeeps and trucks. And I am convinced that the four corners area is a highly occult area.

"The only stretch of highway, namely Highway 666, runs through the four corners area from southeast Arizona to North-western New Mexico and up [and into SW Colorado and SE Utah]. I have also heard that this Highway 666 came into existence around 1947 or 1948, fairly close to the time of 1947, the modern-day beginning of OVERT UFO APPEARANCE, i.e. the Kenneth Arnold incident, and coincidentally or not, the establishment of Israel in 1948."

(Norio believes that the establishment of the nation of Israel in 1948 began the countdown to the final apocalypse -- see Revelation chapter 12, for instance. - **Branton**)

The following is a transcript of parts of a speech presented by Mr. Hayakawa at the 11th LOS ANGELES WHOLE LIFE EXPO held at The Los Angeles Airport Hilton Convention Center on November 16 and 17, 1991. The transcript from which we will quote is a revised and expanded version of the address or lecture written on June of 1992 and titled: *UFO'S, THE GRAND DECEPTION AND THE COMING NEW WORLD ORDER*:

"...AREA 51 is located in the northeastern corner of a vast, desolate stretch of land known as the Nevada Test Site [a large portion of which includes the Nellis Air Force Test Range] but has practically nothing to do with underground nuclear testing. It is located approximately 125 miles north-northwest of Las Vegas and consists of Groom Lake and the Papoose Lake Complexes. The presently expanding eastern portion of the latter complexes is known as the S-4 site.

"This entire area is under the strictest control of Airspace R-4808N [with unlimited 'ceiling'], prohibiting any entry therein of air traffic, civilian or military, unless special clearance for such entry is secured well in advance. By land, the area is meticulously patrolled 24-hours a day by several tiers of external security even though it is conveniently 'covered' by the... Jumbled Hills [...which cover north of the Papoose Lake area], making it virtually impossible for anyone to see the facilities without first climbing atop the hills of the rugged mountain range which became off-limits to the public since 1985.

"The main external perimeter security is now being handled by Wackenhut Special Securities Division, part of the operations of Wackenhut Corporation, a worldwide semi-private security firm based in Coral Gables, Florida which has an exclusive contract with the U.S. Department of Energy and handles not only the perimeter security at the Nevada Test Site but also at many other secret facilities and sensitive installations through-out the U.S. and U.S. interests worldwide, including ground-level perimeters for several large underground facilities in and around Edwards Air Force Base in Southern California.

"It is also important to mention that dozens of unmanned, miniature-sized remote-controlled automatic security vehicles constantly patrol the immediate perimeters of the S-4 Site, located around [and presently expanding particularly towards the eastern portion of] Papoose Lake. These automatic, miniature sized four-wheel vehicles have been produced by Sandia Laboratories of Albuquerque, New Mexico exclusively for the Department of Energy.

"The outer northeastern perimeters of this area located in the Tickaboo Valley come under the geographical jurisdiction of Lincoln County and are relegated to the Bureau of Land Management [B.L.M.]. Yet it is considered highly inadvisable for anyone to even enter the main country dirt road, known as the Groom Road, which begins its southwestern extension towards Groom Lake from a point midway between mile marker 34 and 33 on Highway 375, and leads to the guard shack located two and a half miles northeast of the Groom Lake complexes.

"The first line of exterior security forces [dressed in military-type camouflage uniforms but with no insignia of any kind whatsoever] consists of the GP patrols [the Groom Proper patrols, in Bronco-type four-wheel drive vehicles] who sometimes drive around at night with their lights off on various country dirt roads adjacent to the outer demilitarized zone, intimidating any civilian vehicle that tries to enter those access roads [off of Highway 375] located on public land.

The GP patrols themselves [part of Wackenhut Special Securities Division], however, are strictly ordered to avoid any direct contact with civilians. They are only instructed to radio the Lincoln County Sheriff immediately should anyone be spotted driving on any of those dirt roads. The most common radio frequency used between Security Control and Lincoln County Sheriff's patrols is 138.306 MHZ.

"The only area allowed by the Sheriff for such curiosity seekers to congregate is an open area near a black mailbox located at the south side of Highway 375 between mile marker 29 and 30. Even then, the Sheriff patrol will routinely stop by during the evening to check on the cars parked at the mailbox area.

"Moreover, it is our understanding, based on information provided by a highly reliable source connected to a special U.S. Navy SEAL operations center, that the mailbox area is constantly being monitored by high-powered, state-of-the-art, infra-red telescopes set up at a facility known as Security Control high atop Bald Mountain [10 miles west of the area], the highest peak in the Groom Mountain Range.

"...It was precisely at 4:45 a.m. on the morning of Thursday, April 16, 1992, that an NBC news crew, dispatched to the area to report on the landing of an alleged super spy-plane known as Aurora on Groom Lake, accidentally succeeded in video-taping the first flight [which we have been calling the Old Faithful] of [a] mysterious object while standing at the mailbox area and looking due south toward Jumbled Hills. The footage, taken with a night-scope vision camera, was broadcast nationally on NBC Nightly News with Tom Brokaw on April 20, 1992. The NBC News reported that it had video-taped a test flight of a new U.S. aerial craft that had definitely defied the laws of physics, and that the news team may thus have taken the first glimpse of the other 'deep black' projects [aside from the Aurora project] being conducted within the confines of the top-secret facility.

"Also in regards to the ongoing program, it is to be noted that usually a day or two prior to significant test flights [i.e., only if the test flight is a significant one, by whatever measure known only to the installation] a vehicle-traffic counter is laid on Highway 93, at approximately a mile and a half north of Ash Springs, right before the juncture of Highway 375. The other counter is set up about a half mile or so west upon entering Highway 375. The obvious question is: in such desolate, less-traveled areas of Nevada, why should there be such traffic counters installed on undivided, lonely highways? It is now my belief that the number of cars being registered that head out west on Highway 375 at such times [particularly in clusters, such as caravans] is relayed to several of the security posts at AREA 51, including the main observation post high atop the previously mentioned Bald Mountain. However, it is very possible that they may now have more sophisticated devices for registering the number of vehicles going through the area.

"The February 21, 1990 expedition was instrumental in the subsequent production of a two-hour documentary program entitled *Saturday Super Special* televised throughout Japan on March 24, 1990 which was seen by more than 28 million viewers on prime time. The entire program dealt with AREA 51 and also the crew's pursuit of an alleged biogenetics laboratory thought to be located just outside of Dulce, a tiny town in northwestern New Mexico, about 95 miles northwest of Los Alamos.

"...The U.S. Naval Research Laboratory...seems to have a Parapsychology Research Unit that coordinates its research activities with DARPA [the Defense Advanced Research Projects Agency]. It is my understanding that some of their activities conducted under the auspices of the Office of Naval Intelligence are being held at locations such as AREA 51.

"ELF [extremely low frequency] wave-emitting devices, scalar machines, electromagnetic beam weapons and highly-defined hologramic projections are just a few examples of the many new types of mind-control weaponry that the government seems to have developed in the past three decades or so. Newest researches on special types of hallucinatory and memory-tampering drugs are part of a growing 'arsenal' that the U.S. Naval Intelligence boasts to have developed in its own Parapsychology - Mind Control Unit.

"According to recent information provided to me by a highly reliable informant within a special operations group of the Department of the Navy [D.O.N.], two of the most widely used devices will be R.H.I.C. [Radio Hypnotic Intra-Cerebral Control] and E.D.O.M. [Electronic Dissolution of Memory]. The first of the two, Radio Hypnotic Intra-Cerebral Control, calls for the implantation of a very small, electronic, micro-radio receiver. It acts as a Stimulator which will stimulate a muscle or electronic brain response. This, in turn, can set off a 'Hypno-programmed' cue in the victim or subject, which would illicit a pre-conditioned behavior. The second one, Electronic Dissolution of Memory, calls for remotely-controlled production within the brain of Acetyl-Choline which blocks transmission of nerve impulses in the brain which results in a sort of Selective Amnesia. According to this source, in the hands of certain units within the intelligence community both of these methods are ALREADY BEGINNING TO BE USED!

"An amazing article appeared in the Los Angeles Times on May 12, 1992 announcing that Caltech scientists have recently discovered and confirmed the presence of 'tiny magnetic particles in the brains of humans, similar to those that have heretofore been found in other animals.' [**L.A. TIMES**, Section A, page 3]. According to the Caltech researchers, it is now an undeniable fact that every human brain contains a tiny natural magnetite particle, even from the time of conception. Could the government, particularly the U.S. Naval Research Laboratory, have known this fact for a long time? The answer definitely seems to be in the affirmative!

"It is interesting also to note that as of this writing, many strange, turquoise-colored antenna-towers with triangular configurations on top, are beginning to be constructed along key areas near the freeway systems of many U.S. cities, particularly proliferating the Los Angeles and Orange County areas of California. According to several reports, these antenna-towers are presently being used as relay towers for the increasing networks of cellular telephone systems and are being operated by such firms as Pacific Bell and Telesis.

"Yet the most interesting aspect of the constructions of these strange antenna-towers is that there are increasing reports that the Department of Defense is somehow involved in this operation. The frequency waves being utilized in the cellular telephone communications are, according to several researchers, strikingly close to the range of frequency waves used in several ELF emission and microwave experiments of the U.S. Naval Research Laboratory as well as D.A.R.P.A., the Defense Advanced Research Projects Agency. Will these towers be utilized throughout the nation?

". . .In the meantime, government-sponsored genetics researchers and bio-technology experts at New Mexico's Los Alamos National Laboratory are said to be conducting secret, in-depth studies, not only on the total effects of mind-control projects upon human behavioral patterns, but also on its possible applications relative to such areas as genetics engineering and exploration of the human genome.

(This may be of special interest considering the news in early 1997 out of Edinburgh, Scotland of the successful cloning of an adult Ewe lamb. There are some who contend that certain technological breakthroughs are allowed to leak out into the public domain only after that technology has been harnessed and used for years by the secret scientific fraternities who serve the agendas of the military-industrial elite.

It is interesting that following the announcement of this discovery a Jesuit priest made the rounds on the talk shows defending this 'new' science and advocating the various 'benefits' that it could provide. It is interesting that Adam Weishaupt who founded the Bavarian Illuminati was a Jesuit; and it is also interesting that the Scottish Rite of Masonry originally had its origin within the Jesuit college of Clermont in France. - **Branton**)

"A large underground genetics laboratory is thought to be located just outside of Dulce, a tiny town in the midst of the Jicarilla-Apache Indian Reservation located about 95 miles northwest of Los Alamos and 100 miles east of [the] sinister-sounding Highway 666, the only stretch of highway in the U.S. with that designation and the only highway that links the four states of Arizona, New Mexico, Colorado and Utah.

"Perhaps it may just be a pure 'coincidence' that this highway -- befittingly named Highway 666, which originated in southeast Arizona and goes up north, cuts into northwestern New Mexico, right near the Four Corners area, an area that happens to have one of the most consistently concentrated UFO sighting reports in the country since around 1947. This entire Four Corners area, especially northwestern New Mexico and southwestern Colorado [even extending, for that matter, to the entire southern tip of the state] also has had some of the most concentrated reports of unexplained cattle mutilations in the nation during the late seventies and early eighties. Was something covertly taking place in those areas?

"Even though we could not locate the alleged underground genetics laboratory in Dulce when the Nippon Television crew and I visited the area in late February of 1990, I had several opportunities to interview scores of local residents there that admitted seeing nightly appearances of mysterious lights – [occasionally accompanied by unmarked black helicopters] darting over, into and out of nearby Archuleta Mesa and Archuleta Mountains.

"Many of them even claim to have spotted, on many occasions, military-type trucks and jeeps as well as government vans passing through Dulce and loitering around nearby mesas. Occasionally even black limousines carrying what appeared to be 'CIA' agent-types were claimed to have been sighted loitering around the foothills of other nearby mesas.

"We must bear in mind that the Dulce area is only 95 miles northwest of Los Alamos. Los Alamos National Laboratory is one of the top U.S. research laboratories specializing in the study of the human genome. Also it is a vital center of the government's SDI research and development programs.

"Just about a hundred miles southeast of Los Alamos is Albuquerque, New Mexico's largest city, and more significantly, a city where Kirtland Air Force Base is located right next to the sensitive Manzano Storage Facility, a top-secret underground military facility [where nuclear warheads are stored]. Sandia Corporation, one of the nation's top-secret government contractors specializing in top military-industrial projects, is also located in Albuquerque.

"As far as advanced bio-technology is concerned, I have no doubt that a micro-chip implantation technology is being perfected in which tiny micro-chips could be implanted in our circulatory systems, vital organs and tissues if need be for whatever purpose the future may 'require'. It is my conclusion that a large-scale research has been completed by the government [with possible assistance from 'outside' sources] within the last 20 years or so utilizing tens of thousands of cattle in the Southwest to conduct this covert experiment. Only recently has science proven that cow hemoglobin could be substituted [by utilizing a special purification system] with human blood in situations of 'unforeseen national emergencies.'"

Chapter Six
Cosmic Top Secrets and the Dulce Base

The Sept. 10, 1990 issue of *UFO UNIVERSE* related the following under the title-heading, "WILLIAM F. HAMILTON III -- UFOLOGY'S MYSTERY MAN TO REVEAL COSMIC TOP SECRETS":

"Until just recently, William F. Hamilton III managed to keep up a relatively low profile so that he can continue his work in private and without needless interruption from well-meaning, and never-the-less prying eyes.

"Admittedly, his name is not known in every household, but the fact of the matter is that Bill is highly respected among his peers.

"Indeed, what he has to say is as important and vital as the words of flying ace John Lear and former Navy intelligence officer William Cooper, who have gone on record regarding the alien conspiracy.

"In fact, much of what Hamilton maintains is consistent with the theory that there is a massive government cover-up on UFOs and alien visitations that reaches right up to the President's private office door, and that the U.S. military has made a secret pact with a group of aliens known as the Greys. [They] are on earth...mutilating cattle, and abducting humans for experimental purposes. Supposedly the Greys have TAKEN OVER several Top-Secret underground military facilities, AND certain branches of the government [who] are working hand-in-hand with these entities to bring about total domination of the world, while a SECOND group of extra-terrestrials is here trying to protect us...

"Of a highly controversial nature, many of Hamilton's statements may seem overly 'radical' to even his closest associates, not to mention other investigators who refuse to even seriously consider the documentation he is able to present to bolster his case.

"...About ten years ago, a few scientists and engineers, who worked for NASA and shared an interest in UFO abductions, came together to form a group they called Project VISIT -- Vehicle Internal Systems Investigative Team. They studied about 130 cases of UFO abductions with the goal of constructing a model of UFOs, their operation, and the entities who crew UFOs.

"They found: UFOs have bright interior lighting. Abductees undergo a medical-type examination with apparently highly sophisticated equipment. Burns are suffered by many abductees. Time loss - from 20 minutes to 3 hours - is common. Project VISIT member, Dr. Richard Niemtzow, described the crew members as four feet tall, hairless, grey in color, with no nose, a small mouth and large slanted eyes. The Grey humanoid is emotionless and communicates by telepathy.

"The Greys have earned a reputation quite different than the Nordic blondes and other reported species. Most of the abductions are done by Greys and more than one variation of Grey. The Greys do most of the biological intervening on abductees. Tans, Whites, and Blues (i.e. 'Greys' of other skin colors, gray-tan, gray-white, gray-blue, etc. - **Branton**) have also been reported by abductees. I have personally had some sort of encounter with what I call the Whites. They are small with extremely white skin and black, wrap-around eyes.

"EARTH MADE SAUCERS – In April, 1984, Lt. General George Bone, Vice Commander of the U.S. Air Force Systems Command was killed while test flying a secret aircraft over the Groom Lake area, a top secret facility located about 100 miles north of Las Vegas, Nevada. This facility is designated Area 51. The Systems Command reputedly uses this facility to test-fly spy planes, such as the SR-71 Blackbird or its successor, the Aurora.

"According to the February, 1988 issue of *GUNG-HO* magazine which ran a feature article on Area 51, some of the craft being flown out of that test facility would make George Lucas drool!

"In the early 1980s a radio technician working at Area 51 reported seeing a saucer on the ground. It was some 20 or 30 feet in diameter, he said, and when it flew, it moved silently through the air. The technician also viewed a number of wooden shipping crates marked **Project Redlight.** That project may have been a forerunner of Snowbird. Presently, the Air Force is trying to acquire 89.000 acres adjacent to the Groom Lake facility and to place the nearby Groom Mountains off-limits to the public.

"Before and after the TV documentary *UFO COVER-UP LIVE*, there had been talk of an underground alien base located in the vicinity of the Groom Lake test site, known as Dreamland. . . This adds a whole new dimension to the idea of a secret space program and hints at fantastic secret programs that take [us] more than one step beyond.

"A friend of mine once moved to Riverton, Wyoming to escape from terrifying mysteries he encountered in NEW MEXICO. He said the locals at Riverton asked him: 'Are you here to work on the secret space project out at the jet airport?' Saucers were seen close to the ground in Riverton. One day my friend's truck broke down and he had to hitch a ride to town. A black Lincoln pulled up and a man dressed in black gave him a lift. The dashboard looked like a computer console. The MIB knew exactly where he wanted to be left off in front of the post office, but my friend had never told him.

"ALIEN IMPLANTS -- In 1980 when I lived in Glendale, Arizona, I received a call from my friend Walter Baumgartner, who published a magazine of limited circulation called ***ENERGY UNLIMITED***. Walter was a natural technologist. He said that he had started working for a physicist by the name of PAUL BENNEWITZ at Thunder Scientific Labs in Albuquerque, New Mexico. He then proceeded to tell me the fantastic story that Mr. Bennewitz had succeeded in communicating with aliens at an underground base situated near MT. ARCHULETA in the town of DULCE that was close to the Colorado border and situated on the Jicarilla Apache Indian Reservation. (Note: Bennewitz actually stated that he interrogated the alien-collective via a computer-radio-video link with an alien computer terminal, by tapping-in to the aliens' ship-to-base communications frequency and using a type of hexedecimal mathematical code to break the alien encryption. He first discovered the signals using specialized equipment he had developed, and later concluded that these signals were also being used to influence abductees who had been given electronic mind-control implants. - **Branton**).

"He told me that these little grey aliens were abducting and implanting people with a device inserted at the base of the skull for the purpose of monitoring and CONTROLLING humans. He said that the government knew about this and was involved with alien activities. He also stated that the aliens feared our nuclear weapons and nuclear radiation. He told me that Paul was working on a weapon that would be effective against these aliens.

(INTERJECTION BY BRANTON REGARDING MIND CONTROL IMPLANTS: I know of a person who went to have some implants removed by doctors. The implants were removed, via the nasal cavity, from the nerve centers of the brain – some of her nerves were damaged in the process. This nerve damage resulted in a near-death experience following which, when she had awakened, she felt like a 'new person' or that some other 'identity' that had been operating in her was now gone. Some mystics may refer to alien intelligenc's that possess human minds as 'walk-ins.' What many refer to as 'walk-ins' are often artificial intelligence matrix implants which are attached to the nerve centers of the human brain. These serve as 'nodes' for an alien collective in a parasite-host capacity, allowing the aliens to physically utilize the human subject after an altered state of consciousness has been induced, and the human subject's individual consciousness is incapacitated.

This transfer to the 'alternate consciousness' often occurs at night. Also, both malevolent and relatively benevolent other-worldly cultures often induce within human subjects one or more 'alternate' personalities which are taught or programmed to work and operate in the other realm. If the individual is left-brain dominant and right-handed in their conscious life, in the 'alternate' life they may be right-brain dominant and left-handed, as is the case with my own elusive alternate identity.

Other than saying that humans have one brain with two hemispheres, it would be just as legitimate to say that we have two brains in one cranium. In many cases where more benevolent humanoids are concerned, the individual may have flashes of memories of a double or 'alternate' existence where they interact with exterran, subterran or even other-dimensional humanoid societies, often in an intimate capacity, and in some cases even serve as starship crew members or pilots.

In the case of the benevolent non-interventionists, such an alternate personality may be a means of interacting with Terrans without violating the laws of non-intervention and interfering with an earth-persons conscious life, although I myself would suggest that even this would be stretching 'non-interventionism' to the limit. However in the case of the malevolents, such alternate identities are programmed through intense mind-control techniques with the intent of producing unconscious mind-slaves for the alien collective.

The secrecy and fear of the exposure of their interventionist agendas is in this case the motive for maintaining secrecy. What is especially confusing however is when one, as in my own personal case, has been infused with alternate personalities or identities by BOTH benevolent AND malevolent other-worldly cultures.

The Dulce Wars

In my personal case this involved being patched-in to an alien collective-mind [Ashtar] via implants and used by the dark side of that collective – or the interventionist elements within the Ashtar collective such as the 'Orionite infiltrators' that some contactees have spoken of who desire to use their positions to establish absolute control – only to later have this or another alternate personality matrix re-programmed by a more benevolent faction of the alliance. This more benevolent faction would either be involved with a separate Federation, or it would be a faction that is part of the collective itself yet which is involved in an ongoing conflict with its 'darker' side, a faction which is opposed to the interventionist-control agendas of the infiltrators.

One cannot comprehend the significance of the psychic battles that can rage through a single human mind until one has been caught in the crossfire between two OPPOSING alternate personalities – one of which is an individualist and one of which is a collectivist – that are slugging it out for dominance of ones unconscious existence.

The best one can do in such an event would be to try and retrieve as many suppressed memories as they are able, sort the whole mess out, and assimilate and take conscious control of those thought patterns that will be most beneficial to them and eliminate the harmful thought-patterns. I will not deceive you, such a process can be very painful at times. After all, it is the ROOT "individual consciousness" of a human being which has the final say as to just WHO that person is going to be, based on the universal law of free agency.

For those of you who are reading this and who feel that they may have been 'programmed' with an alternate 'alien' personality which is activated during alien encounters, I will say for an absolute fact that according to universal law this collectivist alternate personality MUST submit to the demands of your conscious will. Anything else would be a direct violation of the non-intervention laws. Even without the assistance of alien psycho-technology, certain psychiatrists are fully aware of how easy it is to hypnotically induce an alternate personality within a human being, IF they had access to the suppressed mind-control techniques that have been used by certain intelligence agencies and occult fraternities. (For further information about mind control and implants, be sure to read *Mind Stalkers* by Commander X, and published by Global Communications. - **Branton**)

The Dulce Wars

"UNDERGROUND BASES – On April 1 and 2, I spent 24 hours visiting with John Lear at his home in Las Vegas. He took out a stack of papers and had me peruse them at my leisure. His study room had walls covered with aircraft photos and certificates. There was no doubt in my mind that John loved flying. John is a soft spoken individual and frequently, while visiting him, I have watched him putter in the garden. We discussed Area 51. John had some long distance photos of the Groom Lake facility. The one thing that stood out in one photo was the radio telescope pointing straight up in the midst of a group of buildings. The scope was probably tracking any overhead spy satellites.

"He showed me the reference in the February, 1988 issue of *GUNG-HO* magazine, that [insisted] that spacecraft were being test-flown from this facility. John heard rumors that the Greys had a base under the Groom Mountains. This is the one we believe is called DREAMLAND.

"One of my sources [a leak] says DREAM is an acronym that stands for Data Repository Establishment And Maintenance. John told me the story of Mr. K, whose son Robert was trapped inside a joint human-alien underground base in Utah. This Robert had apparently worked at DULCE BASE at one time. MR. K felt like he was being given the run-around by the military in his attempts to locate his son.

"I learned that there were a few technical people who worked at Sandia Labs in Albuquerque who were interested in alien activity. One man I talked to, C.R., knew a mysterious Colonel Ronald Blackburn, who was reputed to have said that there were 600 aliens at the Groom Lake facility in Nevada. C.R. had investigated a UFO crash near Gallup, N.M. in 1983. This one was also investigated by Tommy Roy Blann. I heard of Colonel Edwards at Albuquerque who knew the AFOSI agent Richard Doty (BOTH of whom worked with Paul Bennewitz in his investigations of the alien activity taking place at the Dulce Base. - **Branton**). Doty had talked to some investigators about the government cover-up. Why? I don't know.

"WEIRD HAPPENINGS AT DULCE – On April 19, 1988, my wife and I arrived at Dulce, N.M. at about 4:30 p.m. Dulce was a beautiful little mountain town sitting at an elevation exceeding 7,500 feet. There was still snow on the ground by the Best Western Motel. I checked into the motel and called Gabe Valdez. He came over to see me about 9:30 p.m. We talked about UFOs and the cattle mutilations. He said that he had not seen any mutes since 1981-82. [I] had him read a letter written by Richard Doty in which Doty denies all involvement with UFO secrecy. He said Doty wasn't telling the truth. This proved true, because Doty started talking again.

"He told me that Doty wrote a report that stated that Paul Bennewitz was being investigated. Later Gabe offered us a ride around Dulce. He took us in his patrol car and showed us some of the routes. He said he saw glowing orange-lighted airships flying silently around the area frequently. He never saw these airships in daylight. We took a look at the Gomez Ranch, site of some of the mutes that took place in 1978.

"We asked about Bennewitz's belief that there was a secret underground alien base in the area. He said he believed about 80 percent of what Bennewitz said concerning alien activities in the area. . . he definitely seemed to think there was a base in the area, but his idea of where it is located was different than Paul's. He thought that the base might be south of Dulce, closer to the Gomez Ranch. He said he had not found any entrances to the base. He had found landing tracks and crawler marks near the site of the mutes. He invited me to come back sometime and climb Mt. Archuleta. Someday I would come back to Dulce, but I had no idea when...

"A lot started happening in October, 1988. I started investigating the case of a couple who had gone up to a plateau on the south side of the Tehachapi Mountains. At two in the morning they witnessed a large flashing orb come up from the ground and rise slowly into the sky. They experienced about two hours of missing time. Under hypnosis performed by a local hypnotherapist who had taken an interest in UFO abductees, we had found that the man recalled having been taken to an underground facility. He kept mentioning 'the Colonel!'"

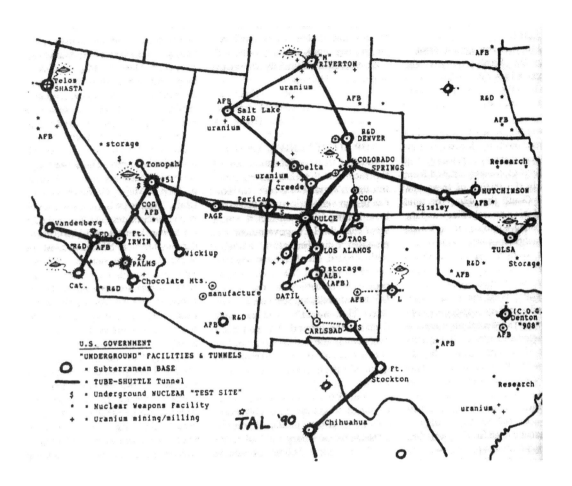

Here is a top secret map of various underground alien bases and the tunnel systems that connect them--as released to *UFO UNIVERSE* by UFOFORCES director Bill Hamilton and Tal.

The Dulce Wars

Chapter Seven
Probing Deeper into the Dulce Enigma

The following information on subsurface anomalies and the Dulce base was compiled by researcher and explorer John Rhodes:

Legends from different parts of the globe all tell of an underworld inhabited by mystical beings of varied forms. I believe that the reptilian [race] still resides to this day underground, hidden away in the dark crevices of the Earth and in the depths of the oceans. The evidence supporting this proclamation is also available through recent reports and historical documentation.

In the early 1960's, a subterranean nuclear blast occurred about 30 miles southwest of Dulce, New Mexico right off U.S. 64. This nuclear blast was conducted under the umbrella of project Plowshare, and was named Gassbuggy. It has recently been alleged that this particular subsurface nuclear blast was used to create a hollowed out chute or chimney for development of a substation for a super-secret tunnel system attached to an underground black book project base.

According to the infamous Thomas Castello – a former Dulce base security technician – this particular under-world city is a highly secret base operated by humans as well as reptilian aliens and their worker cast, the commonly encountered Greys. It is here, apparently, that a multitude of experimentation projects are carried out. Primarily genetic experiments on kidnaped men, women, and children.

In 1961, Castello was a young sergeant stationed at Nellis Air Force Base near Las Vegas, Nevada. His job was as a military photographer with a top secret clearance. He later transferred to West Virginia where he trained in advanced intelligence photography. He worked inside an undisclosed underground installation, and due to the nature of his new assignment his clearance was upgraded to TS-IV.

He remained with the Air Force as a photographer until 1971 at which time he was offered a job with RAND corporation as a Security Technician, and so he moved to California where RAND had a major facility and his security clearance was upgraded to ULTRA-3. The following year he met a woman named Cathy.

The Dulce Wars

They married and had a son, Eric. In 1977 Thomas was transferred to Santa Fe, New Mexico where his pay was raised significantly and his security clearance was again upgraded. . .this time to ULTRA-7. His new job was as a photo security specialist in the Dulce installation, where his job specification was to maintain, align and calibrate video monitoring cameras throughout the underground complex and to escort visitors to their destinations. Once arriving in Dulce, Thomas and several other new 'recruits' attended a mandatory meeting where they were introduced to the BIG LIE, that: "...the subjects being used for genetic experiments were hopelessly insane and the research is for medical and humane purposes."

Beyond that, all questions were to be asked on a need to know basis. The briefing ended with severe threats of punishment for being caught talking to any of the 'insane' or engaging in conversations with others not directly involved with one's current task. Venturing outside the boundaries of ones own work area without reason was also forbidden and, most of all, discussing the existence of the joint Alien/U.S. government base to any outsider would generate severe and, if necessary, deadly repercussions.

Thomas did his job as his superiors demanded. At first his encounters with actual Grey and reptilian beings in the base were exhilarating, but soon he became acutely aware that all was not what it appeared to be. Thomas slowly began to sense that there was an underlying current of tension existing between some of the personnel and himself. Once in a while he would walk around the corner, interrupting serious discussions between coworkers and, as Thomas was a security officer, these talks would die off into a short murmur and individuals would part company.

One particular part of his job was to go into various areas of the base and align the security monitoring cameras when it was necessary. This afforded him the opportunity to venture out and witness things that would stagger the imagination. Later he was to report seeing laboratories that investigated the following: Psi studies; Advanced mind control analysis and application; Human brain memory recognition, acquisition, and transfer; Matter manipulation; Human/alien embryonic cloning; Rapid human body replicating by use of energy/matter transfer [complete with an individual's memory from the computer memory banks] and other scientific advances.

The Dulce Wars

Once in a while Thomas would see some of the horrifying genetic creations that were housed in separate sections of the base. These, he knew, couldn't have had anything to do with mental illness or health research. Thomas didn't want to look any further. For every time he discovered more pieces to this underground maze, it became more and more overwhelming to accept. His curious mind, however, implored him to search for the truth regardless of his own desire to turn away in horror.

One day, Thomas was approached by another employee who ushered him into a side hallway. Here he was approached by two other gentlemen that whispered the most horrifying words... the men, woman AND CHILDREN that were said to be mentally retarded were, in fact, heavily sedated victims of ABDUCTION. He warned the men that their words and actions could get them in big trouble if he were to turn them in. At this, one man told Thomas that they were all observing and noticed that he too was 'uncomfortable' with what he was witnessing. They knew that Thomas had a conscience and they knew they had a friend.

They were right, Thomas didn't turn them into his commanders. Instead, he made the dangerous decision to quietly speak with one of the caged humans in an area nicknamed "Nightmare Hall."

Through their drug induced state, he asked their name and their home town. Thomas discreetly investigated the claim of this 'insane' human during his weekends out of the facility. He discovered through his search that the person had been declared missing in their home-town after vanishing suddenly, leaving behind their traumatized families, who followed dead ends and trailed flyers. Soon he discovered that MANY of the hundreds, perhaps thousands of men, women and children [from ALL AREAS OF THE WORLD] were actually listed as missing or unexplained disappearances.

Thomas knew he was IN OVER HIS HEAD and so were several of his co-workers. All he could do, until somehow the situation changed, was to be alert and extremely guarded with his thoughts. The Grey aliens' telepathic capabilities allowed them to 'read' the minds of those around them and if he revealed his intense anger, it would be all over for him and his new friends.

In 1978, tensions within the Dulce base were extremely heightened. Several security and lab technicians began to secretly sabotage the genetic experiments.

The Dulce Wars

Increasingly frail nerves and paranoia finally erupted into what is commonly referred to as the Dulce Wars. It was a literal battle between the Reptilians and the humans for the CONTROL of the Dulce base. It was the Reptilians more than the humans that were pushing the "Big Lie," and insisted on using humans in their experiments, AND those who did not survive the experiments [were used] as 'sources' for the liquid protein tanks which 'fed' both embryonic Grey fetuses as well as full grown Greys, as a source of nourishment. It was a horror beyond the capability of the human mind to comprehend. The initial "Dulce War" conflict began on Level Three.

No one is exactly sure how it started, but we do know through Thomas' account that it involved the [base] SECURITY FORCES armed with beam weapons known as "Flash Guns", machine-gun toting [U.S. Military] personnel, and the Grey alien species. When the smoke cleared, sixty-eight humans had been killed, twenty-two were completely vaporized and nineteen escaped via the tunnels. Seven were recaptured and twelve remain in hiding to this day. Thomas returned to his post awaiting the planning of his own escape.

(Note: It is not known just exactly how many grays were killed in the conflict, but it is obvious that the human security personnel were far outnumbered by the aliens since literally thousands of Greys worked in the lower levels of the Dulce base, according to Castello. There are indications that the 'spark' may have occurred when many of the scientists within the lower levels – who had learned about the "Grand Deception" of the aliens and their LIES concerning the abductees – were captured by the Reptilians and apparently confined deep within peripheral bases underneath the Ute Mountains of SE Colorado and SW Utah. A few others apparently escaped and told those in the upper levels what was happening below. The Greys/Reptoids could not afford to let escape the fact that they had VIOLATED the treaty with MJ-12, and in fact had been violating it ALL ALONG with NO INTENTION whatsoever to keep it. They had hoped that the humans would not become wise to their "Trojan Horse" operation until they were able to infiltrate the planet more completely. At least 100 special forces were sent in by superiors who were ignorant of the whole picture in an effort to rescue the scientists and maintain order and control of the base, however the aliens – who far outnumbered and out-teched the human forces, managed to kill 66-68 of them. - **Branton**)

The Dulce Wars

In 1979 the intense pressure that was brought upon Thomas in his job finally made him break the code of silence. He told his best friend, by a hand passed note, that he was working in a sub-surface, huge installation outside of Dulce, New Mexico.

He told his friend that he was working side by side with Grey aliens that consider themselves native Terrans and that the upside-down black triangle with the inverted gold colored T inside it was the insignia of the project.

Thomas knew that he had to leave the job for his own peace of mind, however now that he knew the truth about the abductees being held below, it would be almost impossible to live a 'normal' life. He would always be under observation and threat until the day he died. He also was aware of the fact that old age may not be his downfall. His demise could easily be expedited by certain individuals. After one of his weekends away from the facility, he decided to return to work. This time through one of the less guarded air shafts, unannounced and into the base by way of secret passages. Once inside, he preceded to appear as if he was working his normal duties while taking charge of every thought as he passed by Greys. During this time inside the base, he removed still photographs of the facility and treaties signed, with authentic signatures, between California Governor Ronald Reagan, several other individuals and the Greys. Thomas also managed to retrieve a 7 minute black and white surveillance video of genetic experiments, caged humans, Greys, as well as schematics of alien devices and complex genetic formulas. These items, he felt, were not only his chance to a seat at the bargaining table when the need arose, but also they were things that the public needed to know about.

He made copies of the films, photo's and paperwork, packed several 'packages' and instructed several different people who he trusted explicitly to bury or hide them until the right time.

He was then made aware through certain sources that his wife, Cathy, and son, Eric, had been forcibly taken from their home to an undisclosed underground facility for 'safe holding' until he decided to return with the items. At this point, he knew that even IF he did return everything to the Dulce commanders, that his wife and son were probably NEVER going to be the same again [if returned at all] after being manipulated by aggressive mind control. He also knew that he AND his entire family would most DEFINITELY become permanently missing due to some tragic accident. Thomas was at zero option. He quickly dissolved into a lonely life on the run. From state to state, border to border, motels to sofas, always looking behind him and trying his best to look ahead.

There are a myriad of other specialty science projects taking place at the Dulce base including, but not limited to: Atomic manipulation, cloning, studies of the human aura, advanced mind control applications, animal/human crossbreeding, visual and audio wiretapping, the list goes on.

Dulce, New Mexico is a strange place indeed. It's a sleepy little town perched upon the Archuletta Mesa, just south of the Colorado border in northern New Mexico. Tourists passing through sometimes see little more life in the town other than that of a scruffy dog lazily spread out along side of the dirt road. Some claim that upon entering the town, black vehicles with heavily tinted windows tailgate them until they are outside the city limits and "heading out of Dodge!"

In addition, several other sources, who wish to remain nameless, reported oddities in their work with operation 'Plowshare' during the 1960's. The project was created under the guise of the use of atomic bombs during peacetime, and forged ahead under the umbrella of "Natural Gas Exploration." In fact, several of these multi-kiloton blasts were used as a rapid way of developing huge sub-surface chambers for facility development. It is reported that the technology to clean radiation is available and already in use for such projects.

When I lectured on Friday, August 13th of 1993 in Las Vegas, I made public, for the first time ever, the floor plans to levels one and six of the Dulce Base. These floor plans were reproduced from the originals that were handed to Thomas Castello's friend. This friend did not previously release the floor plans because they were being used as a verification device to the claims of abductees that say they were there. To date, the originals have verified and disproved many stories circulating the field of UFOlogy. This friend of Thomas Castello's, however, believes that it is time to begin [to] reveal the missing pieces.

The Dulce base floor plan was illustrated as per the originals by Thomas Castello and I released it. . . during my lecture in Las Vegas, Nevada. Its layout, when inspected carefully, appears to be extremely strategically planned. From a vertical viewpoint, it resembles a wheel with a central hub and corridors radiating outwards like spokes. This 'hub' is the focal point of the entire base. It is surrounded by central security and extends through all levels of the base. I believe this core to be the Achilles heal of the entire facility. It probably contains fiber optic communications and power lines. This would justify its highly guarded and central location as well as explain its vertical continuation through all levels. With all communication lines and power lines focused towards the hub, it is possible that any one level could be completely "locked down" by its own security or the security hubs from either above or below its own level. This would provide maximum control over the entire facility.

The 'spokes' or corridors radiating away from the central hub, lead to numerous other labs in five different directions. Connect the spokes and a pentagon is revealed in its design. From above, this base resembles the layout of the Pentagon in Washington D.C. complete with halls, living quarters, cafeterias and military insignias on the walls.

When viewed laterally, its appearance takes on the look of a tree with a trunk at its center and its floors extending outwards like the branches. If this is a facility of science, then one could easily say that its lateral appearance is like that of the tree of knowledge. Was this purposely designed this way or does it just happen to be a coincidence?

The overall design of this facility reminds one of a multi-stacked subterranean Hopi Indian kiva. Although I believe that it's somewhat of a disservice to the Hopi to even be spoken of in association with a cave of horrors like the Dulce base, its similarity in design should not be forgotten.

As cultures around the world tend to bring their own styles of architecture with them during periods of migration, so perhaps did the advanced civilization that 'originally' built [the] Dulce Base. If the reptilian influence over man is as great as archaic documentation and myth would have one believe, then there have to be other subterranean dwellings similar to this in other locations.

Chapter Eight
A Dulce Vanguard at Deep Springs?

It has been fairly well established that the Dulce, New Mexico network is the largest and most significant alien [Reptoid/Grey] base network in North America. However according to one source there is also another 'nest' near Deep Springs, California.

This [Dulce-connected?] base – because of its proximity – may pose an even greater threat to the humanoid residents of the subterranean network who have major city-complexes below California: Mt. Shasta, Panamint Mountains, 29 Palms area, etc. These colonies are reportedly being contested by 'Draconian' vanguard positions near Lakeport-Hopland, Mt. Lassen and Deep Springs, California.

On the other hand, some of the non-interventionists 'Nordic' cultures reportedly have their own forward positions near the Four Corners or Colorado Plateau region where the Reptoids/Greys have their major center of activity. Then there are other areas BETWEEN the two sectors [between the Andro-Pleiadean bases centered under Death Valley and the Draco-Orion bases centered under Archuleta Mesa] where the collaborators meet.

There are basically three alien networks at work on earth: The Anti-Grey Nordic [Federation] factions, the Anti-Nordic Grey [Empire] factions and the Nordic-Grey collaborators, which would also include those Terran intelligence agencies and occult lodges who are involved in the collaboration for whatever motive.

Even within the collaboration, there is a great deal of struggle over whether the humanoid or Reptoid agendas should have the upper hand. Within the collaboration itself 'speciesism' [akin to racism] exists at certain levels, so in spite of the species prejudices the collaboration continues nevertheless because of a 'marriage of convenience.'

In other words the Greys want to take over the planet and impose a slave society to ultimately serve their empire, but they need the Illuminati's international economic connections to do so; and the Illuminati wants the same thing but they realize that they need the alien mind-control and abduction technology to accomplish their goals.

The Dulce Wars

So then, it is more of a love-hate relationship. They collaborate in order to set up a planetary government, however both the Humanoids and Reptoids are constantly plotting for the time when the world government arrives so that once it is established they can move-in and take full control and expel the necessary collaborators – the humans doing away with the Greys or the Greys doing away with the humans or whatever the case may be.

For instance the Illuminati might negotiate with the Greys while at the same time develop SDI weapons to potentially use against them. On the other hand the Greys may continue negotiating with the humans while at the same time implanting micro-electronic mind-control devices in the human agents with whom they negotiate in order to ensure that they remain under ALIEN control once the planet succumbs to the New World Order. So a one world government will NOT bring peace to the planet, it will merely be a matter of fighting for control of one super-government rather than for many smaller ones.

What many do not realize is that there appears to be a third element behind this agenda, a 'race' of paraphysical entities that some might refer to as the 'Luciferians' or the 'Poltergeists' – who are often described, by abductees who have encountered them, as being in the appearance of quasi-physical etheric or energy beings who have often been seen overseeing and directing the actions of the humanoid-reptoid collaborators.

Although it might sound simplistic to imply that this cosmic battle is essentially being fought between the 'Nordic' bases near Death Valley and the 'Grey' bases near Archuleta Mesa, the true fact of the matter is that when we are dealing with multi-levelled subterranean systems the border zones are a little more complex than on the surface, where we have obvious horizontal borders between countries.

In 'inner-planetary' warfare the 'battle-lines' are horizontal, vertical and in some cases inter-dimensional. The battle would be one that is being waged above, below and within our society, even though the outward manifestations of that 'war' might not be immediately seen for what they are, unless one is aware of the REAL conflict behind the scenes. There are also indications that at least CERTAIN factions of the NSA-MJ12-CIA-AVIARY agencies have 'defected' from the neo-Nazi New World Order agenda of joint interaction with the Reptoids/Greys, and are now AT WAR with the same.

The Dulce Wars

Recently a researcher with the initials K.S., was approached by the family of a U.S. Intelligence worker [O.S.I.] by the name of 'Tucker', who had disappeared mysteriously. The family was concerned and frightened as they had discovered, in a personal locker of his, SEVERAL papers describing INTIMATE details of activities surrounding the Dulce, New Mexico and Nevada [S-4, etc.] underground installations. Several of these papers are reproduced throughout this present work. Among this large stack of papers was hidden the following letter which was stamped SECRET. The letter, copies of which were apparently also in the hands of a few other researchers as well, stated the following:

"Dear John...

"I am writing to you in the event that I do not return.

"There is a triangle surrounding the Nevada Test Site.

"There are in fact two of them. Each one frontiers on the other. One is the ELECTRO-MAGNETIC TRIANGLE, installed by MJ-12. This is a shield to protect the 'Benevolents' [very human looking] from the EBEs (the so-called 'Extraterrestrial Biological Entities' or Greys - **Branton**) while they help us develop our counter-attack/defenses. The other is the EBEs' trap keeping the Benevolents in the redoubt. . . At each corner of the EM Triangle you will find BLM stations and they are the transmitters of the shield.

"Facing each one of these is an EBE transmitter... THERE ARE MANY OF THESE STAND-OFFS THROUGHOUT THE WORLD. It is important that you do not interfere by attempting to destroy one of their 'surrounds', they would be able to 'double-up' somewhere else and overthrow that position. Once that link is over-thrown, our support team would fail. Their over extension is deliberate on our part. We are like the Chinese, we can't out technology them but we can out number them. Especially since they can't breed here and it is too far for them to go back home without our help. Many of our EM Triangles are ruses to keep them over extended. They can't get out of our solar system because the electromagnetic field (at this time? - **Branton**) is the wrong frequency for their propulsion system to work efficiently. This massive 'field of energy,' completely surrounds the neighborhood of planets around the sun. This explains why the EBEs can not commit more vehicles to our solar system."

There have been comments among some contactees to the effect that occasionally the solar system passes through areas of differing electromagnetic variations as it moves in and out of cosmic energy streams that flow through the universe like a vast universal electromagnetic circulatory system. Certain energy fields are conducive to certain types of propulsion systems whereas others are not, and in these cases alternate or more conventional forms of propulsion must be resorted to.

Some even suggest that large ships disguised as asteroids, planetoids or even comets are being used by the Greys and Reptoids in order to get around this propulsion problem and also to conceal their presence. These 'engineered' planetoids are accompanied with conventional drives to serve as platforms for various operations: abductions, implantations, mutilations, and also mind control and infiltration activities taking place on or under planet earth.

All of this would seem logical, so as not to attract a great deal of attention and in return resistance from the masses. Some of these converted 'planetoids' have been identified as Geographos, Phobos, and even Hale-Bopp comet – which was accompanied by many unusual anomalies not observed in most comets.

It would seem that a Federation of Worlds, based in the Andromeda and Pleiades constellations, is attempting to 'blockade' the interventionist actions of the Draco-Orion empire in the Sol system. According to contactees these Federation forces will soon be joined by a massive fleet from Sirius-B, who are apparently Federation allies who have [let us hope] severed themselves from a large segment of the Ashtar collective which has since been infiltrated and taken-over by Orion-based Reptoids and Greys.

These Andro-Pleiadean backed Sirians have reportedly waged, and won, a civil war in Sirius-B with the dark side, or the renegade Ashtarian collaborators. They are now reportedly en route to the Sol system to do battle with the Draconian-Orion forces and to convince the renegade Sirian collaborators who are working with them that they have and are being misled into an interventionist agenda. Like fanatical cultists, the rebel Sirians have blindly succumbed to the deceptions of the Reptilians, Greys and the Rebel Angels who are controlling the infiltrated segment of the Ashtar collective and are masquerading as "ascended masters" of the Ashtar command. At least this is what some contactees have implied. Are these contactees relaying the truth? I would guess that time will tell.

As for the humans at the Nevada Test Site, these "may" be in fact – if we are to believe the collective revelations within this volume – victims of subtle reptilian propaganda and intimidation. For instance, this source who authored the letter about the EBE's apparently believes that ALL of the Saurian-Greys or EBE's come from extra-terrestrial realms. However as we have indicated, there is much evidence suggesting that reptoid or homosaurian activity exists deep within the subterranean cavernous levels throughout planet earth, an intra-terrestrial presence that has existed for many centuries if not for thousands of years.

This is one fact that the Reptoids have tried to hide from humankind, both terrestrial and extraterrestrial. Also, there are accounts suggesting that the Reptoids and Greys ARE IN FACT breeding profusely and reproducing themselves via deep subterranean polyembryony, cloning and incubation facilities below Dulce and elsewhere and are not as over-extended as they might have us to believe. Some estimate that at the very least 20 million Greys are now actively operating under the surface of planet earth within bases or within natural cavern systems. According to still others, 20 million is a conservative estimate.

However, on the other hand, the fear the humanoids might have of prematurely attacking the enemy positions may possibly be the result of intimidation and propaganda intended to keep humans from taking OFFENSIVE action, believing that they are keeping the Greys, etc., at bay when in fact the Greys ARE ATTACKING OFFENSIVELY HUMAN SOCIETY on several other hidden fronts via mass abductions, subliminal programming, implantation, psychic manipulation, recruiting of fifth column human agents, and infiltration. I personally do not believe in standoffs.

In war there is no neutrality, one is either attacking [in various ways] or capitulating themselves over to the enemy, in various ways – ways which those on the defensive side might not even be aware of. The letter which we have quoted earlier continues: "The headquarters of this particular surround is Deep Springs, California. At this location one can find a school for right-wing extremists who have defected to the EBEs in exchange for an 'Aryan-ruled world,' and a promise to allow them to enslave what they consider to be a subhuman world population. Their sperm fertilize eggs taken from abductees. You will not likely see the hybrids hidden inside the mountain, unless you have nightscope binoculars. Some human APPEARING malevolents [mercenaries] are also there. The human traitors don't realize that they are being 'used' by the aliens to further their secret goals.

"One will also find that each corner of their triangle is at the base of a mountain. At each location you will find several entrances to underground systems. Do not attempt to enter, unless you wish to become liquid protein. You may however harass the EBEs' two other corners by placing a large magnet on the vaults... [placing a magnet on the other two entrances at each location will not affect anything]. This temporarily interrupts their communications with Deep Springs until a collaborator team comes out to see what is going on.

"If you place a large magnet on this entrance [it has a large computer near the surface, you can hear it], it will affect an immediate interruption. So, you can take it off in a short time [1 hr] and take it with you. They will still have to come and reset the system. If you plant magnets [camouflaged like rocks] around these entrances, the EBEs won't come out & the sell outs won't be able to find them.

The EBEs are also allergic to high concentrations of sugar (and apparently other substances with a left hand atomic spin, it has been claimed. - **Branton**). You will find that at two locations I have poured sugar around their exits. Always wear magnets near these locations, they interrupt the EBEs' sense of direction [due to an internal compass much like those found in migrating birds] similar to our loss of balance when our ear drum is affected.

"Please wait until I have returned, if you have an airplane, I would like to take aerial photos, we can photograph them together.

"Our alliance crest, symbolic of the EM Shield, and our sign/mark/graffiti is enclosed. Do not reveal them or else everybody will use them & you won't know the real from the pseudos.

"YOU DO NOT KNOW ME, I DO NOT KNOW YOU. THIS IS NOT FOR PUBLIC DISSEMINATION. ZEALOTS MAY DISRUPT THE BALANCE BEFORE V-EBE DAY." Another researcher by the name [pseudonym] of Jason Bishop has revealed that 'John,' to whom the letter was addressed, is none other than John Lear who himself claims many connections with people 'in the know' who go right to the top. According to the letter, both the Nevada Test Site and Deep Springs are areas of conflict between a U.S. Goverment - 'Nordic' Alliance AND a Socialist - Reptoid [Grey] Alliance.

Jason Bishop also released some other information he received by way of John Lear, from the individual whose letter we've just quoted. According to Lear, the author of the letter was actually a Security Officer at the Test Site who had called-in to the Billy Goodman talk show [KVEG radio - Las Vegas, NV] on a few occasions, before Goodman went to Southern California to take over a more lucrative talk show position.

This person used the codename: Yellow Fruit, which he claimed was actually the codename for a top secret security division that worked at the site, with which he was involved. YF also sent to Lear a copy of the Benevolent teachings.

The Benevolents are reportedly working at the Test Site with MJ-12 and are Blond-Nordic and/or Aryan-like people. I would personally guess that the Benevolent Ones are members of the exterran Andro-Pleiadean Federation and/or members of the subterranean Telosian-Agarta Alliance which has maintained ties with the ASHTAR collective, or in this case the non-collaboration faction of that collective.

The BENEVOLENT TEACHINGS [not limited to the below] were identified as follows:

"DISCOURAGED – NON PREPARATORY SPORTS [Activities That Can Not Be Used In Non-sporting Life] motocross, auto-racing, skateboarding, roller skating, football, baseball, hockey. Also Discouraged: Processed Sugar, Recreational Carbohydrates, Recreational Fluids, White Bread.

"ENCOURAGED – NONCEREMONIAL LESSONS OF THE MAJOR RELIGIONS & PREPARATORY SPORTS [Activities That Can Be Used In Nonsporting Life] swimming, running, hiking, martial arts, survival arts. Teach Your Children!

"FORBIDDEN – Alcohol, Illegal Drugs, Nicotine, Recreational Drugs, Unjustifiable Homicide.

"MUST – Avoid Weakness [evil grows in weakness]. Execute Evil Prisoners In Order To Help Other Prisoners (Editors Note: Another possibility that might be interjected here is to establish a completely secured underground prison-cave and place all of the worst offenders there and leave them to themselves, to either work out their problems or destroy each other, whichever they choose. **Branton**).

"MUST – Quarantine Contagious Disease Victims Humanely. Show Strength. Stop Illegal Drugs. Stop Destruction of Environment. Stop Pollution.

"STUDY - Bill Of Rights, Biology, Computers, Economics, Geography, History, Latin, Mathematics, Philosophy, Survival Skills, United States Of America's Declaration Of Independence, United States Of America's Constitution, Vocational Skills."

Yellow Fruit also provided coordinates for the Electro-magnetic Triangles he referred to in his letter. These include: N 37 22 30 - E 117 58 0; N 38 21 0 - E 115 35 0; N 35 39 0 - E 114 51 0; also Yucca Lake: N 37 0 30 - E 116 7 0.

The following information, from William F. Hamilton III, describes further details on the "Yellow Fruit" account – including claims which the Nevada Test Site agent made over the air during the few interviews which were heard over KVEG Radio's Billy Goodman talk show.

It is also interesting that COM-12 member Michael Younger [who has given lectures on the Nazi presence within the Rockefeller-backed Oil companies – Nazi war criminals and their families who were smuggled into America following World War II and given refuge within the Rockefeller's corporate empire; the plans the Nazi's/Bavarians have for selling-out the planet to the aliens in exchange for one quarter of the New World Order; and a MASSIVE Nazi child abduction & satanic-ritual-sexual abuse & murder ring operating within ARCO, etc.] is or at least was at one time also a worker at the Nevada Test Site. This suggests that COM12 is intimately involved in the counter-offensive against the Greys.

"...Yellow Fruit revealed that A CONFLICT WAS GOING ON BETWEEN THE BENEVOLENT ONES and THE EBE's and that now the benevolent ones had gained the upper hand at Dreamland where he said a contingent of 37 benevolent ones were stationed and where three EBE's were held in captivity.

"Bizarre! Science Fiction? Could these amazing and disturbing stories possibly be true or not? Yellow Fruit knew a lot about the test site area. I resolved to go to the location he gave of the EBE installation in Deep Springs,

California and then on to visit Pat at the Rachel Bar & Grill to make contact with Yellow Fruit [the name for the first level of security force at Area 51 and also the name of an old Army-CIA unit]. The second level of security he called "Sea Spray" and intimated that you would have an encounter of the unpleasant kind if you ever met with them.

"Callers to the Billy Goodman Radio Happening had already organized trips to mile-marker 29 ½ on highway 375 where a dirt road left the highway to intersect the road to Dreamland. There was a heavy black mail box on this road which identified it. I got to Rachel early one October morning and left my card with Pat at Rachel's Bar and Grill to pass on to Yellow Fruit. She knew him by sight. I then inspected the dirt roads where people stood to observe the test flights.

I had already interviewed four witnesses by phone who testified that they had seen UFOs over the Groom Mountains on certain nights in the same area they were seen by John Lear. I made a second trip to the area in late October where a public group visited Rachel and that is when I saw the mysterious Yellow Fruit in the cafe. He later called me on the phone. I left him with a copy of my book, *Alien Magic* and he remarked on the research I had done concerning the search for underground bases.

"According to Yellow Fruit and others there are underground bases and tunnels that conceal the activities of the aliens and secret government projects..."

One more note on the Nevada Test Site - Area 51 - Groom Lake - Dreamland underground facilities: Aside from reports that Dougway, Utah serves as an underground 'link' between Dreamland and DULCE, there is the added claim that another underground link exists farther south, at Page, Arizona.

Anyone who has been to the Glen Canyon dam [Lake Powell] could easily observe how the dam might be used as an entrance to such a base, and how the large hydroelectric facility might power the base operations. The Glen Canyon Dam connection was not specifically mentioned [by former Dulce base security officer Thomas E. Castello who named Page, Arizona as a 'connecting' base], however if there is a base under Page, then it would be logical to utilize this hydroelectric facility in one form or another.

Chapter Nine
An Alien Fifth Column on Earth?

The mysterious "government insider" whose books have been published by Tim Beckley's Abelard Press of New York, "Commander X," related a very interesting incident which involved the subterranean mega-complex beneath Dulce, New Mexico:

"...In another case an old illustrator, John D., does very painstaking work, but while he was on active duty at Dulce he began to act very queerly. He would write letters to the President informing him of a plot underway to undermine the government, and to sabotage the base. He began to draw pictures of American flags, beautifully executed. He drew strange designs of mechanical devices, began to visit the library and bring back books on physics and advanced electronics. He hardly knew how to spell the words.

"He would patiently explain something of a very technical nature which he shouldn't have understood. When asked what he was raving about and why he was causing trouble by writing the President, John D. would say that he had been 'sensitized.'

"'Last year when I was sick [John D. explained], the doctor on the base gave me sulfanilamide. There is a fifth column in this country that is tied up with aliens. Selenium is being slipped into SULFA DRUGS, and this selenium lodges in the bones and makes the body receptive to extremely short waves, those in the wave band of the brain. Similar to the waves that can be detected by the encephalograph. About 300,000 people in this country have been sensitized, and at least seven secret radio stations have been set up in this country, and they are broadcasting to these sensitized persons, instructing them in the best way to perform acts of sabotage against our planet.'"

These claims as given by the Dulce worker, John D., are incredible indeed, and could easily be dismissed as the ravings of a madman, IF NOT FOR THE FACT that many others are saying basically the same thing, that there is a movement underway to bring the minds of the masses under the subjection of an alien force, whether through electronic implantation and control, subliminal programming, or through other means. This movement will use any means. Why would the 'controllers' use the United States as the major target of their activity? We believe that this is due to the fact that the United States is a place that was originally intended by it's 'founding fathers' to be a refuge for peoples FROM ALL NATIONS to come and work out their collective destinies free from the restrictions of prejudice and the oppressiveness of tyrannical rule – a land where all people could express their creativity, culture and individual destinies without interference.

This was their intention, however it is obvious that the 'dream' has not been fully realized because of collective and governmental compromise of the principle that "all men are created equal." The United States, nevertheless, is unlike any other single nation. It is a cultural "melting pot" and a place where not only international human societies on the surface CONVERGE and intermingle in a dramatic way, but apparently where human societies beneath or beyond the earth converge as well.

For instance, according to various reports, most non-surface human societies who are aware of planet earth have their representatives walking among us in our own society [and to some extent, other nations throughout the world], although many of these choose to keep a low profile for either honorable or not-so-honorable reasons. Another factor is the respect which the BILL OF RIGHTS gives to all American citizens, allowing for personal freedom and individuality so long as the freedom and individuality of others is not threatened. Individuality is the MORTAL ENEMY of the alien "Hive," you could say.

The U.S., then, seems to be in essence a "World Scenario," if not a 'universal' scenario in miniature and therefore the 'Conspiracy' sees it as a most valuable prize. Therefore it would probably not be too 'far out' to suggest that the war between the human and serpent races from all three 'realms' [extraterrestrial, ultraterrestrial and intra-terrestrial] CONVERGES within the United States, and to be more exact, within the vicinities of the Archuleta plateau near Dulce, New Mexico [a MAJOR earth-base of the Reptoid interventionist Empire forces]; the Death Valley region of California [a MAJOR earth-base of the Humanoid non-interventionist Federation forces]; and then we have the 'battle-grounds' between the AMERICAN-COM12-CABAL-PHILADELPHIAN-NORDIC and the BAVARIAN-AQUARIUS-MAJI-PHOENICIAN-REPTOID forces within high-security military complexes like those which permeate the underground territories below California, Nevada, Utah, Idaho, Arizona, Colorado, Oklahoma and New Mexico... and apparently centered specifically in or near the underground military-industrial systems beneath Lancaster, California; Mercury, Nevada; Burley, Idaho; Dougway, Utah; Page, Arizona; the underground systems below the Denver International Airport of Colorado; and also below Oklahoma City. All of these basing areas are seen by the proponents of the New World Order as strategic sites that they MUST maintain control of if they are to force America to submit to a one-world government.

The elusive Commander X has – through his reported connections within the Intelligence Community – released still further revelations regarding the dark secrets of Dulce. The Commander claims to be a member of "THE COMMITTEE OF 12" [COM-12?], an obscure intelligence group which is working to educate the public about the joint fascist-alien threat to America and preserve our Constitutional-based Republic as it was established by the original founders of the United States:

"...There were over 650 attendees to the 1959 Rand Symposium. Most were representatives of the Corporate-Industrial State, like: The General Electric Company; AT&T; Hughes Aircraft; Northrop Corporation; Sandia Corporation; Colorado School of Mines, etc.

"Bechtel (pronounced BECK-tul, a San Francisco - based organization - **Branton**) is a supersecret international corporate octopus, founded in 1898. Some say the firm is really a 'Shadow Government' -- a working arm of the CIA. It is the largest Construction and Engineering outfit in the U.S.A. and the World [and some say, beyond].

"The most important posts in the U.S.A. Government are held by former Bechtel Officers. They are part of 'The Web' [an inter-connected control system] which links the Tri-lateralist plans, the C.F.R., the Order of 'Illuminism' [Cult of the All-seeing Eye] and other interlocking groups..."

"MIND MANIPULATING EXPERIMENTS... The Dulce Base has studied mind control implants; Bio-Psi Units; ELF Devices capable of Mood, Sleep and Heartbeat control, etc.

"D.A.R.P.A. [Defense Advanced Research Projects Agency] is using these technologies to manipulate people. They established 'The Projects,' set priorities, coordinate efforts and guide the many participants in these undertakings. Related Projects are studied at Sandia Base by 'The Jason Group' [of 55 Scientists]. They have secretly harnessed the Dark Side of Technology and hidden the beneficial technology from the public.

"Other Projects take place at 'Area 51' in Nevada. . .'Dreamland' [Data Repository Establishment and Maintenance Land]; Elmint [Electromagnetic Intelligence]; Cold Empire; Code EVA; Program HIS [Hybrid Intelligence System]: BW/CW; IRIS [Infrared Intruder Systems]; BI-PASS; REP-TILES, etc.

"The studies on Level Four at Dulce include Human Aura research, as well as all aspects of Dream, Hypnosis, Telepathy, etc. [research]. They know how to manipulate the Bioplasmic Body. They can lower your heartbeat with Deep Sleep 'Delta Waves,' induce a static shock, then reprogram, Via a Brain-Computer link. They can introduce data and programmed reactions into your Mind [Information impregnation -- the 'Dream Library'].

"We are entering an era of Technologicalization of Psychic Powers... The development of techniques to enhance man/machine communications; Nano-tech; Bio-tech micro-machines; PSI-War; E.D.O.M. [Electronic Dissolution of Memory]; R.H.I.C. [Radio-Hypnotic Intra-Cerebral Control]; and various forms of behavior control [via chemical agents, ultrasonics, optical and other EM radiations]. The Physics of 'Consciousness.'

"SURVIVING THE FUTURE... The Dulce Facility consists of a central 'Hub.' the Security Section [also some photo labs]. The deeper you go, the stronger the Security. This is a multi-leveled complex. There are over 3000 cameras at various high-security locations [exits and labs].

"There are over 100 Secret Exits near and around Dulce, many around Archuleta Mesa, others to the source around Dulce Lake and even as far east as Lindrich.

"Deep sections of the Complex CONNECT INTO [EXTENSIVE] NATURAL CAVERN SYSTEMS.

"...INSIDE THE DULCE BASE... Security officers wear jumpsuits, with the Dulce symbol on the front, upper left side (the Dulce symbol consists of an upside-down triangle with an inverted 'T' superimposed over it - **Branton**). The ID card [used in card slots, for the doors and elevators] has the Dulce symbol above the ID photo. 'Government honcho's use cards with the Great Seal of the U.S. on it. 'The Cult of the All-Seeing Eye' [The NEW WORLD ORDER], 13, '666', The Phoenix Empire... '9', 'Illuminism'... 'One out of many.' [and so on]..."

The Dulce Wars

"THE PHANTOM BOARD: ABOVE THE LAW... Most meetings of 'The Dulce Board' are held in Denver and Taos [New Mexico]. A former U.S. Senator has full knowledge of Dulce. He was among the group that included a number of very prominent government figures who toured the base (i.e. most likely the upper levels only - **Branton**). In 1979, an 'animal mutilation' conference took place in Albuquerque, New Mexico. This meeting was used to locate researchers and determine what they had learned about the link between the 'mute' [i.e. mutilation] operations and the 'Alien' government.

"Another Senator knows about the 'Ultra' secrets at 'Dreamland' and Dulce. Several of my official sources have confirmed this to me. So do many others in government... this is what the UFO researchers are up against...so be careful. You know more than they want you to know.

"They have also underwater bases off the coast of Florida and Peru.

"More detailed information will be released in the near future: photos, video tapes, documents, etc. Watch out for 'Special Agents' among you now.

"In the 1930's, DIVISION FIVE of the FBI knew about the 'Aliens.'

"A FASCIST cabal within this country had John Kennedy assassinated. Look to the links within the larger Umbrella... the 'WEB' of a fascist totalitarian secret police state... within the Pentagon; JCS, DIA, FBI [Division Five]; DISC/DIS and the DIA. Note: The Defense Investigative Services insignia is a composite of the Sun's rays, a rose and a dagger, symbolizing 'The Search for Information, Trustworthiness and Danger.'

"This links with caves used for 'Initiation Rites' all over the world... ancient vaults, retreats, [underground 'bases']..."

Commander 'X' also stated that: "Recently, participants in a field investigation of the area near Archuleta Mesa, were confronted by two small hovering spheres. They all became suddenly extremely ill and had to quickly leave the area.

"We have passed the point of no return in our interaction with the 'alien' [i.e. 'reptilian grey'] beings. We are guaranteed a crisis which will persist until the final REVELATION [or conflict].

"The crisis is here, global and real. We must mitigate or transform the nature of the disasters to come, and come they will. Knowing is half the battle. Read the book, *THE COSMIC CONSPIRACY*, by Stan Deyo."

The Dulce Wars

Chapter Ten
The Deep Dark Secret at Dulce

The Feb.-Mar. 1991 issue of *UFO UNIVERSE* carried an article titled 'THE DEEP DARK SECRET AT DULCE', written by Bill Hamilton and 'TAL' LeVesque. If planet earth is to be the central 'battleground' or staging-ground for a final cosmic battle between galactic superpowers, and if the U.S. is one of the major areas on earth where the 'final outcome' will be decided, and since the Dulce, New Mexico area is considered to be THE MAJOR BASING SITE where human - alien collaboration AND/OR conflict is taking place, then we should focus our attention on what has been going on deep beneath this small southwestern town.

More than any other area in the U.S., if not the world... this small town has been the epicenter for nearly every form of paranormal activity one can imagine, including: UFO sightings, UFO landings, Abductions, Implantation's, Human & Animal mutilations, PSI Warfare studies, Secret Government-Alien interaction, U.S. 'Constitutional' Government vs. Alien Agenda conflicts, 'Reptilian' sightings, Cryptozoological or Bioengineering phenomena [this was the general area where the famous 'Cabbit,' the half cat / half rabbit was captured], Underground bases, Conspiracy scenarios, Alien Infiltration, Deep-Cavern phenomena, Super High-Tech activity, & MIB encounters.

In fact a higher CONCENTRATION of such activities has been evident in the vicinity of Dulce than any other area in the world, to the point that the inhabitants of this town have for the most part resigned themselves into acknowledging – although not necessarily accepting – the reality of such activity, whether they like it or not.

Bill Hamilton and 'TAL' Levesque take us 'inside' the Hadean-like labyrinths deep within this underground megacomplex, through the eyes of those who have actually been there, so brace yourselves:

"Dulce is a sleepy little town in northern New Mexico. It's population is about 900 and it is located above 7,000 feet on the Jicarilla Apache Indian Reservation. There is one major motel and just a few stores. It is not a resort town and it is not bustling with activity. Yet, according to a few outsiders, Dulce harbors a deep, dark secret. That secret is said to be harbored deep below the tangled brush of Archuleta Mesa. That secret involves a joint government-alien biogenetic laboratory designed to carry out bizarre experiments on humans and animals.

"New Mexico State Police Officer Gabe Valdez was drawn into the mysteries of Dulce when called out to investigate a mutilated cow on the Manuel Gomez ranch in a pasture 13 miles east of Dulce. Gomez had lost four cattle to mutilations between 1976 and June 1978 (and SEVERAL more in ensuing years. - **Branton**) when a team of investigators which included Tom Adams arrived from Paris, Texas to examine the site of the carcass.

"Curious as to how cattle were being selected by the mysterious mutilators, an interesting experiment was conducted on July 5, 1978 by Valdez, Gomez, and retired scientist Howard Burgess. The three penned up about 120 of the Gomez beef cattle and moved them through a squeeze chute under an ultra-violet light. They found a 'glittery substance on the right side of the neck, the right ear, and the right leg.' Samples of the affected hides were removed as well as control samples from the same animals.

"Some investigators attribute the mutilations to aliens from UFOs. Sightings of strange lights and other aerial phenomena have been reported in many areas where the cows have been found at the time of the reported mutilation. UFOs have been seen frequently around Dulce.

"I arrived in Dulce on April 19, 1988, to visit with Gabe Valdez and to inquire about the sightings, the mutes, and the rumors of an underground alien base in the area. There was still snow on the ground by the Best Western motel when I checked in and called Valdez. He made an appointment to see me at 9:30 PM. I found Gabe to be a very congenial host as he offered to show us around the roads of Dulce that night and point out the various locations where he had found mutilated cows or had seen strange aerial lights. He made the astounding statement that he was still seeing unidentified aircraft at the rate of one every two nights. We took a look at the Gomez Ranch, the road by the Navajo River, and the imposing Archuleta Mesa. Gabe had found landing tracks and crawler marks near the site of the mutes. Gabe was convinced that scientist Paul Bennewitz of Thunder Scientific Labs in Albuquerque was definitely on the right track in his attempts to locate an underground alien facility in the vicinity of Dulce.

The Dulce Wars

"I had first heard of Paul Bennewitz in 1980 when my friend Walter called me from Albuquerque and told me he had been working with Paul on electronic instruments. Walter said Paul had not only photographed UFOs, but had established a communication link with their underground base at Dulce. Bennewitz had first come to prominence during the August 1980 sightings of UFOs over the Manzano Weapons Storage Area and Kirtland AFB.

"A KIRTLAND AFB INCIDENT REPORT dated October 28, 1980 mentions that Bennewitz had taken film of UFOs over Kirtland. Paul was president of Thunder Scientific Labs adjacent to Kirtland. Bennewitz gave a briefing in Albuquerque detailing how he had seen the aliens on a video screen (via a computer-radio-video link he had developed using a hexidecimal code after tapping-in to their ship-to-base communications frequency, Paul himself being a brilliant scientist who has developed equipment for the Space Shuttles and several Fortune 500 companies. - **Branton**). The aliens were transmitting signals... from a base underneath Archuleta Mesa.

"Researcher William Moore claims that government agents became interested in Bennewitz' activities and were trying to defuse him by pumping as much disinformation through him as he could absorb. Whether Paul's communication with supposed aliens at the Dulce Base was part of this disinformation campaign is unclear. If one were to believe that Paul is the SINGLE source of reports on the Dulce Facility, then it could also be a tactical maneuver to discount and discredit Paul's allegation of an underground base if such reports were meant to remain secret. Then the actual disinformation maneuver would be to dis-inform the public and NOT a single individual.

"In a report entitled 'PROJECT BETA', Paul states that he had spent two years tracking alien craft; that he had constant reception of video from an alien ship and underground base viewscreen; that he had established constant direct communications with the aliens using a computer and a form of Hexadecimal code with graphics and printout; and claims to have used aerial and ground photography to locate the alien ships' launch ports and charged beam weapons.

Paul claimed that the aliens were devious, employed deception, and did not adhere to agreements. Paul and Walter were working on a weapon that would counter the aliens. Some will think at this point that we have crossed-over from the land of clear thinking concerning anomalous phenomena to the land of science-fiction. But let us remember that bizarre phenomena such as the UFOs represent may have its roots in a bizarre reality. It is expected to be bizarre at first, but as we continue our studies we will evolve to understand it.

"Paul Bennewitz had investigated the case of abductee Myrna Hansen of New Mexico who reported having been taken to an underground facility in May 1980. Christa Tilton of Oklahoma has reported that she had an experience of missing time in July 1987 where she had been abducted by two small Grey aliens and transported in their craft to a hillside location where she encountered a man dressed in a red military-like jump suit.

"She was taken into a tunnel through computerized check-points displaying security cameras. She reported having been taken on a transit vehicle to another area where she stepped on a scale-like device facing a computer screen. After the computer issued her an identification card, she was told by her guide that they had just entered Level One of a seven-level underground facility. Christa goes on relating how she was eventually taken down to Level Five. She reports having seen alien craft and little Grey alien entities in some of the areas that she passed through.

"Christa reports going into one large room where she saw large tanks with computerized gauges hooked to the tanks and large arms that extended from some tubing down into the tanks. She noticed a humming sound, smelled formaldehyde, and was under the impression that some liquid was being stirred in the tanks. Christa has made drawings of much of what she had witnessed during her abduction.

"These tanks Christa talks about were depicted in a set of controversial papers called the *Dulce Papers*. These papers were allegedly stolen from the Dulce underground facility along with 30 black and white photos and a video tape by a mysterious security officer who claims to have worked at Dulce up until 1979, when he decided that the time had come to part company with his employers. The rest of the story is about this security officer who has met with one of us in an attempt to tell us the truth about the aliens, the [so-called] U.S. Government, and the Dulce base. He announced his intention to come out of hiding and present soft and hard evidence of his claims. Unfortunately, he has disappeared along with the alleged evidence. It will be up to you to decide whether the remaining evidence shows that a government cover-up exists.

The Dulce Wars

Chapter Eleven
A Dulce Base Security Officer Speaks Out

The following is a list of questions that were directed to former Dulce Base Security officer Thomas Edwin Castello approximately a year before his death [or disappearance]. They are followed by his responses:

QUESTION - When exactly was the [upper human-occupied level of the] Archuleta installation constructed?

ANSWER - I heard Dulce was started in 1937-38 by the Army engineers, enlarged over the years, most recent work was completed 1965-66 to connect tunnels to the Page [Arizona] Base, site of one of the older underground facilities. The four corners base is called PERICA. Most of the Native Americans [the Indians] living in that area are aware of that base, and could tell us about the underground life forms that frequently are spotted near those communities, Bigfoot, etc. (Note: The references to the Dulce base here deal mainly with the upper levels, not the extreme lower levels which include vast natural caverns and, some believe, very ancient tunnel systems as well. This would include the tunnels illuminated by phosphorus pentoxide which the alien grays avoid, and the origin of which is unknown. In fact sources have informed us that some of the underground NORAD facilities of Colorado were constructed within already-existing cavern systems, suggesting that Ray Palmer and Richard Shaver were correct when as early as the mid-1940's they wrote about the government's search for ancient underground cave and tunnel systems to be converted for their own use. - **Branton**)

Q – By what means were the [upper] installations constructed? Are you familiar with the alleged developments made by the Rand Corporation of a highly-efficient bore or mole machine capable of melting rock using nuclear powered wolfram-graphite tipped 'drill-cones'?

A – According to several senior maintenance workers, part of it was blasted by nuclear devices in the sixties. There are sections, like the shuttle tunnels, that were formed by an advanced tunneling machine that leaves the tunnel walls smooth. The finished walls in those tubes resemble polished black glass.

Q – By WHOM was the Dulce installation originally constructed?

The Dulce Wars

A – Nature started the caverns. The Draco [reptilian humanoids] used the caverns and tunnels for centuries. Later, through RAND Corporation plans, it was enlarged repeatedly. The original caverns included ice caves and sulfur springs that the aliens found perfect for their needs. The Dulce caverns rival Carlsbad caverns in size. (Note: Carlsbad caverns and especially the adjacent Lecheguilla caves are 'officially' among the largest and deepest in the world, with several leads that remain to be explored by professional speleonauts - **Branton**)

Q – Are the various electromagnetically-controlled air or spacecraft – [that have been seen] leaving from and arriving at Mt. Archuleta – manned by humans, the alien entities, or both?

A – Archuleta Mesa is a minor area... the craft leave [and are stored] in five areas. One is SE of DULCE, one near Durango Co., one at Taos, N. M., and the main fleet is stored at LOS ALAMOS [under].

(Note: I believe Thomas Castello is referring to the joint-operational fleet. From combined sources however it appears as if Dulce is absolutely SURROUNDED ON ALL SIDES by alien bases, and that Archuleta peak, although apparently the central NEXUS of the entire underground network, is nevertheless just one part of an overall complex that some claim is nearly the size of Manhattan!

One source has indicated that there are chambers a few hundred feet below the very town of Dulce itself that are part of level one of the facility. This close proximity may explain why it has usually been described as the Dulce Base. Apparently even with his high-security clearance, Thomas Castello was only familiar with one part of the overall mega-complex which underlies the area. Whatever amount of activity is taking place there, different sources seem to indicate that the town of Dulce nevertheless lies over a major crossroads, convergence or intersection area of alien activity even though the core of alien activity has been extended to Los Alamos.

Los Alamos and the mountainous regions east and southeast of it in and around the Santa Fe National Forest seem to be the MAJOR nest of Reptiloid/Gray forces in North America, although there is also a large number of dens scattered throughout the underground networks between Dulce and Area 51. Dulce seems to be a major through point for exterran and subterran reptilian activity, a central infiltration zone for surface operatives, as well as an operational base for abduction-implantation-mutilation agendas and also a major convergence for sub-shuttle terminals, UFO ports, and so on. - **Branton**)

Q – Others have suggested that some of the entities below Dulce are not of extraterrestrial ORIGIN, and that they are actually descended from saurian or reptoid beings such as the Velociraptors or Stenonychosaurus Equallus – a serpentine race or races similar to that hinted at in the third chapter of the book of Genesis?

A – Yes, some Reptoids are native to this planet. The ruling caste of aliens ARE reptilian. The beige or white beings are called The Draco. Other reptilian beings are green, and some are brown. They were an ancient race on Earth, living underground. It may have been one of the Draconian beings that tempted Eve in the Garden of Eden. Reptoids rightly consider themselves native Terrans.

Perhaps they are the ones we call the Fallen Angels. Maybe not, either way, we are [considered] the squatters on Earth.

Q – Some have suggested that the so-called underground E.T. bases and tunnels may, for a large part, be literally thousands of years old... constructions of an antediluvian race which attained to a considerable level of scientific complexity, and who were destroyed by a Divinely-initiated cataclysm which took place after they attempted to merge their science with occult/supernatural forces. For instance some have suggested that the Bermuda Triangle phenomena may be the result of an out-of-control Atlantean experiment that led to a space-time disaster which produced electromagnetic fallout in the Triangle area and elsewhere after they had accidentally loosed powerful forces and energies into the world that they knew very little about. Do your observations tend to confirm or refute such a possibility?

A – I'm not sure about the Divine part, but these 'aliens' consider themselves NATIVE TERRANS.

Q – Where do the little Grey aliens fit in?

A – They work for, and are controlled by the Draco. There are other gray skinned beings that are not in league with the Draco.

Q – Did you ever talk to any of the aliens at the Base?

A – Since I was the Senior Security Technician at that base, I had to communicate with them on a daily basis. If there were any problems that involved security or video camera's, I was the one they called. It was the reptilian working caste that usually did the physical labor in the lower levels at Dulce. Decisions involving that caste were usually made by the white Draco. When human workers caused problems for the working caste, the Reptoids went to the white Draconian boss, and the Draco called me. At times, it felt like it was a never ending problem. Several human workers resented the no nonsense or get back to work attitude the working caste lives by. When needed, intervention became a vital tool. The biggest problem were human workers who foolishly wandered around near the OFF LIMITS areas of the Alien Section. I guess it's human nature to be curious and to wonder what is past the barriers. Too often someone found a way to bypass the barriers and nosed around. The cameras near the entrance usually stopped them before they got themselves in serious trouble. A few times I had to formerly request the return of a human worker.

Q – Are there other sites tied-in to the 'shuttle network' other than those which you mentioned, and if so, where are the entrances?

A – WHERE!?! EVERYWHERE! THEY CRISS CROSS THE WORLD AS AN ENDLESS SUBTERRANEAN HIGHWAY. LIKE A FREEWAY, EXCEPT THIS ONE IS UNDERGROUND. . . The subterranean highway in America is like a freeway except it's underground. That highway depends on electric motors [for trucks, cars and buses] for the paved roads, and it is for limited travel. There is another style of transit for freight and for passengers that is for rapid travel. That worldwide network is called the Sub-Global System. It has check points at each country entry. There ARE shuttle tubes that shoot the trains at incredible speeds using a mag-lev and vacuum method. They travel at a speed that excels the speed of sound. Part of your question involves the location of entrances to that base. The easiest way to answer is to say every state in the U.S.A. has them. Frequently, the entrances are camouflaged as sand quarries, or mining operations. Other complex portals are found on military bases. New Mexico and Arizona have the largest amounts of entrances followed by California, Montana, Idaho, Colorado, Pennsylvania, Kansas, Arkansas and Missouri. Of all the states, Florida and North Dakota have the least amount of entrances. Wyoming has a road that opens directly into the subterranean freeway. That road is no longer in use, but could be reactivated if they decide to do so, with minimal cost. It's located near Brooks Lake.

The Dulce Wars

Q – Are there any bases in the state of Utah? (Note: Thomas mentioned several areas surrounding Utah – Colorado, New Mexico, Arizona, Nevada and Idaho, where there are connections, but little on Utah which according to some sources lies directly over one of the largest NATURAL cavern systems in North America, one that is said to reach deep beneath the Western Rockies as well as beneath the Bonneville basin) Have you heard anything about an alleged underground installation within the Wasatch Mountains?

A – Salt Lake, Lake Powell Area, Dark Canyon, Dougway Grounds, Modena, Vernal. All have exits there. Others too.

(Note: There have been many rumors of ancient tunnel systems being intersected during the excavations of sub-basement levels below major industrial and mall areas in downtown Salt Lake City. Various stories surrounding these tunnels include: explorers who have entered the tunnels and never returned; reports of lizard people down in the labyrinths; reports of Greys working with humans on electronic equipment and massive building projects going on in huge caverns beneath the mountains to the east; reports of humans who are part of an Asian-based Agarta kingdom who maintain colonies within the tunnels and caverns below – and who are in conflict with the Reptoids, Greys, and a group collaborating human fascists from a network of massive underground facilities beneath the Neushwabenland region of Antarctica; reports of men in suits having been seen pacing back and forth through large underground chambers carrying uzi machine guns; reports of seemingly bottomless shafts; large tunnels strung with lights that are big enough to drive a semi-truck through; sections of tunnel walls that looked solid yet which one could put their hands through; rooms which emanate a strange greenish phosphorescent glow; abductees who are taken below and encounter all types of aliens; discs that have been seen emerging from the mountains to the east and attacking incoming UFOs over the valley; Dungeons & Dragons fanatics who have been down in the tunnels and tell wild stories of hundreds of miles of maze-like passages; reports of connections to the tunnel systems via the sewer-drainage network especially underneath the downtown crossroads area; reports of alien activity similar to that which has been described in connection to Dulce, New Mexico; and reports of a huge cavern network that reaches beyond the border of the state in all directions – a huge network that connects the underground systems of Nevada with those of New Mexico. There is a famous story which is not openly talked about – there are two versions. . . both may be true.

In one version a Mormon Temple worker penetrated an underground tunnel below the square in downtown Salt Lake City and traveled for some distance through a series of underground catacombs until running into a lizard-like man. The creature attempted to attack him but the man escaped and managed to find his way back to the surface. He began telling other people what had happened and soon afterwards the government arrived in the area and went in and closed off many of the tunnels leading to the sub-basements of the Temple. Presumably there were some heated debates over how much of the underground system this denomination was allowed to control.

A similar dispute apparently occurred to the southwest where the LDS church maintained a large storage facility under Granite Mountain in Little Cottonwood canyon, within the upper levels of a vast network of caverns. Fascist CIA elements and the Grays came in and took control of the larger caverns deeper within the mountain and ordered the vault workers to stay out of the forbidden areas – and stated that the U.S. Government was now using them for National Security purposes and that it was their patriotic duty to maintain the secret.

The other version concerned a custodian who entered a tunnel near the cinemas area below the Crossroads Mall across the street and to the south from the temple square, while excavation was being carried out in a that part of the Mall. The worker entered the tunnel and before long encountered a serpent type man, beat a hasty retreat, and told his fellow workers what he had seen. The FBI and/or the local police soon arrived and sealed the tunnel.

Another story involved a young man who, along with a friend, had used a chain tied to his pickup truck to rip-up a manhole cover in the area near the mall and the Square. They navigated through a maze of sewer passages underneath and came to a shaft that descended in a series of 5 small rooms one below the other, and from the bottom room a tunnel led south into a large chamber wherein they saw a seemingly bottomless shaft, a large southwest tunnel strung with lights and large enough to drive a semi through, and the footprints of some type of three-toed bi-pedal creature.

Other sources imply that early pioneers and settlers of the area who explored these tunnels came in contact with and in some cases even joined with some of

The Dulce Wars

the Telosian-Agharti-Melchizedek-Mayan underground colonies below the Salt Lake Flats, the Salt Lake Valley and the Western Rockies. These subterraneans had formerly established territorial agreements with the Reptoids and Greys before the aliens broke the agreement and begun invading their subterranean lands below the inner mountain west en-masse in the early 1900's.

The treaties were part of an attempt to stave off a possible inter-species conflict, as skirmishes between the Humanoids [Teros] and Reptoids [Deros] within the cavern networks of North America had been increasing since the 1920's, 30's and 40's. Because of a somewhat non-exclusive collective-mind with which these humans interacted, it was decided that one possible way to convert the reptilians into becoming beings of emotion and compassion was to allow them access to the group consciousness.

The Reptoids however, once given access, immediately began taking advantage of the collective and used it to CONTROL the humans on a subliminal basis. The ease with which this occurred may have been enhanced by the fact that the Reptiloids and Greys were already operating as part of a collective or group mind, one which was far more complex than the Ashtar or Astarte collective itself which many of the Agartians depended on.

This suggests that the reptilian collective or HIVE itself is absolutely void of any and all care, concern or compassion for human beings. Individual Reptoids operating distinct from the Draconian collective might however be tamed by other collective-free humanoids in some cases – as some have reportedly been tamed by the Andro-Pleiadean worlds.

If the non-humans could be severed from the collective they might be deprogrammed and reprogrammed so-to-speak and even attain individual awareness and a degree of emotionalism. In such cases it would not be advisable to give these creatures equal standing among humans, and absolute subservience and monitoring should be enforced even if means were found to sever them from the collective mind network.

When dealing with the reptilian forces, unconditional surrender should be first offered, and if this is not accepted than direct military action would be justified especially in light of the many permanent abductees whom the Greys and Reptoids have taken captive [those who are still alive] to their underground systems. Most of the treaties that the humanoids had made with the reptoids 'down under' have since been broken. . . especially following the Groom Wars of 1975 and the Dulce Wars of 1979, during which time much of the underground U.S. base networks [which were funded by American tax dollars by the way] were taken over by the Greys.

Some sources have implied that the aliens took advantage of the chaos especially during the Dulce wars and commenced to invade and conquer several of the older underground colonies. This apparently led to a rift in the Ashtar collective, with many humanoids and hybrids splitting off and joining with the Andro-Pleiadean Federation non-interventionists, and many Reptoids and heartless humanoid agents splitting off and joining with the interventionists of the Draco-Orion Empire.

The Sirius-B system which – aside from Arcturus and Sol – has been the major center of Ashtar activity, has since been shaken by this split between the two opposing Ashtarian factions and war had reportedly raged through the Sirius system for several years, according to some contactees. An apparent reflection of this division is seen within the underground networks of North America between the Pleiadean-backed Sirian humanoids and Orion-backed Sirian Reptoids. Both had maintained operations within the underground levels before the Dulce Wars broke out.

The Dulce wars were just the mere tip of the proverbial iceberg when we consider that the overall events which happened at Dulce had a chain reaction effect throughout this whole sector if not the galaxy. Before the division occurred, the reptoids were invited to take part in peace talks in Telos and elsewhere as an act of good faith, but the Reptoid-Grey collectivists were more interested in expanding their empire and feeding their insatiable appetite for conquest than they were in making peace, although they agreed to peace treaties that they never intended to keep for Trojan horse manipulation purposes.

There is a remnant collaboration such as that taking place in the underground facilities near Paradox Nevada where collectivist Humanoids and Reptoids from Sirius and Sol still maintain a collaboration of necessity – in order to establish a global control system, however a large number of humanoids within the underground systems are at war with the collectivist-interventionist Reptilian infiltrators who would otherwise 'assimilate' these humanoids into their collective through deception, espionage and mind control. Now several contactees like

Alex Collier, Ray Keller, Stan Johnson and others are claiming that the conflicts in Sirius between the Andro-Pleiadean backed Ashtar forces and the Draco-Orion backed Ashtar forces – which were infiltrated and commandeered by Draco-Orion agents – have now spread to the Sol system, as both stellar superpowers have focused on this most strategic system, intent on protecting their respective interests here from being subverted by the other side. - **Branton**)

Q – Does the Mt. Archuleta "shuttle system" connect with a shuttle system which allegedly radiates from Mt. Shasta in northern California?

A – Yes. Mt. Shasta is a major site of Alien - Elder Race - Reptilian Race - Human meetings. Beginning with Grover Cleveland, every President in U.S. history has visited Telos City. Truman was supposed to have visited the Lower Realms as a High Archon on Earth. He was supposed to have met the King of the World, who gave him the Keys to the U.S.A.

(Note: Whether or not the reigning King of the Agarta realms at the time had benevolent or other motives, subjecting America to an outside super-power without Congressional consent would be considered high treason. Although unelected/appointed individuals working within the Executive-Military-Industrial branch of government might choose to do so of their own volition without Congressional or Senatorial consent, such an act cannot apply to the America which is based on the Declaration of Independence, the U.S. Constitution and the Bill of Rights.

There are apparently two nations occupying the United States, the traditional grass-roots America established by the founding fathers and led by the Electorate government, and the fascist Bavarian-lodge-backed underground nation led by the Corporate government which is contesting the original America on its own soil. Some predict an inevitable civil [?] war between the Electorate/Constitutional/Surface government of the U.S., and the joint Humanoid/Reptoid Corporate/National-Global Socialist/Underground New World Order government, which incidentally was bought and paid for by American taxpayers and other unsavory money-making projects.

This war will apparently provoke an armed United Nations / New World Order invasion of the U.S.A. which, according to George Washington's famous vision at valley forge in 1777, will ultimately end with an American victory as a result of Divine Intervention. Something like this may be inevitable if

The Dulce Wars

FREEDOM is to be preserved on this world, and beyond. We should never forget however that the NWO corporate elite and their draconian masters intend to depopulate the surface of this planet AND the underground systems as well. According to one Navy intelligence source the 33-plus Masons [there are allegedly several degrees above the 33rd degree which interact directly with the draconians and are part of the interplanetary initiatory lodges] intend to set the left-wing caverns and the right-wing caverns against each other in order to depopulate the underground realms so that they can impose absolute Bavarian-Draconian global control of both worlds.

The 33+ and higher degrees according to this source intend to ride out the inferno in super-secret fortified caverns while the 33rd and lower degree masons and their respective left-wing and right-wing armies will be left to die in the surface and subsurface wars. It may be that some of the 33+ Masons intend to ride-out the holocaust in their Alternative-3 bases on the moon and Mars, IF those bases are still active.

Remember, the roots of BOTH the left-wing National Socialist AND the right-wing Global fascist agendas trace back to Bavaria. Isn't it interesting that the legendary dragon has TWO wings – a right-wing and a left-wing – both of which are controlled by a single beast? In essence, when it comes right down to it the war is between the Christian based Constitutional Republic of America and the Luciferian-cult-based Socialist empire of Bavaria.

Both the right and left wing movements are Machiavellian extremes created by the Bavarian Black Nobility [Black here being a reference to something hidden that cannot be seen, and NOT skin color] in order to foment global chaos. There are several claims that the collaboration with the Reptilians began with the Luciferian cults of Bavaria, and was later brought into America via the infiltration of the Scottish Rite and the fascist core of the NSA-CIA.

There may have nevertheless been a reptilian presence below North America within the caverns that dates back several centuries, however a MASSIVE reptilian infestation of these underground systems seems to have begun near the beginning of the 20th century. Mt. Archuleta might be considered the capital of the ALIEN segment of the secret [Bavarian-Draconian] New World Order government in America – with the deep underground systems beneath the Denver International Airport being the capital of the HUMAN segment of the secret government. - **Branton**). Truman received assurance to new high tech knowledge, and victory over all enemies on Earth. He then was introduced to Samaza and Khoach, aliens from Bootes and Tiphon [Draco], both reptilian kings or ambassadors. Truman updated the 100 Treaty [that began in 1933] and requested magnetic advance, space knowledge and experiments. Khoach agreed, Samaza partially agreed. He exchanged hostages for genetic experiments and magnetic advance, but vetoed space and beam weaponry.

Q – Is there any truth to the allegations that the CIA/Aliens have established bases on the moon, and also Mars?

A – I've HEARD that too, but I haven't seen proof with my own eyes. The aliens do allegedly have bases on several moons of Jupiter and Saturn. The CIA operates in other COUNTRIES, but I've never heard they operate on other PLANETS (Note: Perhaps we should have referred to the CIA's superior agency, the NSA, whose personnel reportedly pilot the black-budget UFOs between the LUNA and DREAMLAND bases. - **Branton**).

Q – Have you heard any hints or rumors suggesting that there may be lower levels beneath the ULTRA-7 level of the Dulce base, and also, where these might lead to and what they might consist of?

A – YES. Your guess is as good as mine. . . Sure, there was lots of TALK but that doesn't mean it's there. However, I will tell you I saw elevators that were off limits unless you had an UMBRA or higher security clearance. At that base, information is supplied to me at a need to know basis ONLY! [My clearance was ULTRA-7]

Q – Some insist that the U.S./Secret government has developed it's own disk-craft based largely upon top secret antigravity experiments carried out by the Nazi-German scientists during World War II. Have you heard anything referring to this?

A – When I was working in Photo-security, heard a lot of talk, never saw the proof, but once in the Air Force I developed a roll of film that showed a craft LIKE ADAMSKI'S, WITH A SWASTIKA ON THE SIDE. (Note: A letter from 'R.J.M.' of Pennsylvania dated 1-31-91 stated: "...I have a lot of UFO videos. I also have *THE SECRET LAND* [1947]. It shows Bunger's Oasis and says they discovered warm land at the South Pole. One German author claims the Nazis had a photo-finish FIGHT with Byrd. At the end of the movie, it says: 'Byrd's

Intrepid 4,000 met and defeated ANTARCTICA'S TOUGHEST BATTALIONS.' I don't think they were talking about the weather. . ." Another source has stated that there were loses on BOTH sides, and the Battle for Antarctica against the Nazi's Last Battalion – which had fortified themselves in underground bases below the mountains of Neuschwabenland, Antarctica, ended in a stalemate.

Why would Adolph Hitler and Eva Braun commit suicide after Hitler had spent so much energy executing over 5000 Nazi officials whom he 'suspected' were behind his assassination attempt at the Wolf bunker, especially if he had a way out via a secret Nazi South Polar base?

The March 18, 1994 issue of **THE PLAIN DEALER** [Cleveland, Ohio], carried an AP story titled "DOCTORS FIND BURNT BODY COULD NOT BE HITLER'S." Excerpts include: "...French forensic experts say the charred corpse said to be Hitler's is not his body... experts FALSIFIED verification reports ordered by Josef Stalin to APPEASE the Soviet dictator. . . the body is actually that of an unknown German male. [The forensic experts] spent more than two years analyzing the autopsy reports prepared by Soviet coroners in the days following [the] surrender of the Third Reich in 1945. . . the body [said to be Hitler's] had an extra tooth and only one testicle. . . no German doctor who had examined Hitler before his death ever mentioned either anomaly."

This is also interesting when we consider that the well-known abductee, Barney Hill, remembered the following experience under regressive hypnosis as recorded in the paranormal encyclopedia, **MYSTERIES OF MIND, SPACE & TIME**.

Barney and his wife Betty were abducted by gray-skinned humanoids "from Zeta Reticuli." HOWEVER, one of the beings on the craft was described by Barney Hill under regressive hypnosis in the following words which are taken from p.1379 of the encyclopedia: "...another figure has an EVIL face... HE LOOKS LIKE A GERMAN NAZI. HE'S A NAZI. . . HIS EYES! HIS EYES. I'VE NEVER SEEN EYES LIKE THAT BEFORE!" Remember that this occurred nearly 15 years after Europe had supposedly been "de-Nazified."

There seems to be an Antarctic connection with the Dulce scenario as well as other possible Nazi connections: German tourists scouring New Mexico, exploring mines and caves and buying up land and mineral rights just before the outbreak of WWII; the Nazi-connected CIA's involvement and their placement of several Nazi S.S. agents – who had been brought into the U.S. via Project Paperclip – within the Dulce and other underground facilities; the involvement of secret 'Bavarian' lodges at Dulce; and the possible Antarctica-Dulce connection to Alternative -3.[For more information on Project Paperclip and Nazi UFOs, see: *Evil Agenda of the Secret Government*, by Tim Swartz - Published by Global Communications.]

Another interesting connection is the fact that the secret Nazi teams involved in the construction and operation of the underground bases below the mountains of Neu Schwabenland and elsewhere in Antarctica were called ULTRA teams. ULTRA is also the code-name for the DULCE base! Also there seems to be a direct connection between the Dulce base and the Montauk base in Long Island, which was/is[?] reputedly jointly operated by the Draconian Reptiloids, Orion Greys and the Bavarian Thule Society which had backed the Nazi agenda. - **Branton**)

Q – Tom, did you have access to the alien craft? Were you ever inside any of them?

A – Yes, I frequently saw them in the garages, there are quite a few of them. The main fleet is stored at Los Alamos. Yes, I entered several crafts. There were two things that stick in my mind, the odd spongy feeling of the floors, and the unusual pinkish purple color of the lighting. The crew stated the floor becomes ridged in flight, and the purple tint of the lighting changes to bright blue white. The entire inside of the aircraft are scaled down in size, when compared to the average human. The halls were curved and narrow, but some how, when inside it appears bigger than it looks. Certain areas, the outermost sections, almost felt and looked alive. I was never taken up in one.

Q – Can you give me more information on the reptilian race, what do they do on the sixth level? [The area called Nightmare Hall.]

A – The worker caste does the daily chores, mopping the latex floors, cleaning the cages, bringing food to the hungry people and other species. It is their job to formulate the proper mixture for the type one and type two beings that the Draco race has created. The working caste work at the labs as well as at the computer banks. Basically speaking, the reptilian races are active at all levels of the Dulce Base. There are several different races of aliens that work on the east section of level six (No doubt some collaborating Nordic factions included. - **Branton**). That section is commonly called the Alien Section. The Draco are the undisputed masters of the 5-6-7 levels. The humans are second in command of those levels. I had to ARGUE with one large Draconian boss frequently. His name is difficult to verbalize, Khaarshfashst [pronounced throaty kkhhah-sshh-fahsh-sst]. I usually called him 'Karsh,' and he hated it.

The Draconian leaders are very formal when talking to the human race. These ancient beings consider us a lower race. Karsh called me Leader Castello, but it was used in a sarcastical way. However the worker caste is friendly enough, as long as you allow them to speak first. They will answer if you address them. They are very cautious beings, and consider most humans to be hostile. They always seem surprised when they found many of the humans were open and trustworthy.

There is no fraternizing with the aliens off hours. It is forbidden to speak to any alien race [in the halls or an elevator] without a clear business oriented reason. Humans can talk to humans, and aliens can speak to aliens, but that is as far as it goes. At the work site, however, it's different. There is "free speech" in the labs. The camaraderie found in the labs also reaches the computer banks section. In those areas, everybody talks to anybody. However, everything changes the minute you cross the threshold of the hall. Instantly, all conversations become strictly formal. Hard as it was, several times I had to arrest some one, simply because they spoke to an alien. It's a strange place.

Q – Exactly what first made you aware that something was wrong at Dulce? Seems to me that a place as obviously horrible as this one wouldn't need an Einstein to know that this is a CRIME site! What took you so long? Are you the guy who blew the whistle?

A – There are several things you should know about. I took an oath, under the penalty of death, that no matter what I saw or heard I would never divulge the information. Also, I signed a waiver that states I would willingly give up my life if I was found guilty of treason. At the Dulce Base treason is ANYTHING that mentions the details of daily operations at this facility, when outside the confinement of the this base. When I first arrived, a need to know policy was in effect. The story the honchos told us was that this is a Tri-Biotransfer Facility with Advanced Technology, doing secret advanced adventurous methodology for medical and mental gains. Which is a fancy way of saying they do really risky things with human life just to see what would happen. If a medical cure happens, it will be heralded on the surface of the earth as a marvelous new cure, saying it was found after years of research at some well known medical lab. The real story of the cure is never explained. After all, the Dulce Base IS A SECRET FACILITY!

These people are very good at what they do. They do not tell the truth about the unfortunate people that end up in Nightmare Hall. I worked with aliens. With that in mind, you should get the idea of the secrecy and the security at that place.

Yes, I know this was not the usual hospital type job site, but in the beginning I bought the whole package. I was reminded daily by intercom, in the elevators, that "this site does high risk advanced medical and drug testing to cure insanity, please, never speak to the inmates, it can destroy years of work."

I'm sensible, when doctors say don't speak to them, who was I to destroy the delicate situation? But one man some how caught my eye. He repeatedly stated that he was George S. – and that he had been kidnapped and he was sure someone was searching for him. I don't know why he sticks in my mind, I found I was remembering his face, thinking he sure didn't look or sound insane, but many inmates said that.

The next weekend I convinced a friend of mine, a cop, to run a check on the guy, saying I had a run in with him and was curious. I didn't mention the base at all. It was a sickening feeling when the computer confirmed that George S. was missing. What's worse, the cops thought he was just another guy that got tired of the daily grind and split. That was the beginning.

Am I the one that blew the whistle? No. The next Monday, I searched for George, but he was gone. There were no records that explained what happened to him. It was another security officer that came to me saying he and some lab workers wanted an off duty meeting at one of the tunnels, [off the record]. Curiosity took over and I said OK. That night, about nine men showed up. They said they knew they were risking me turning them in but they wanted to show me some things they thought I should see. One by one they showed records that proved many inmates were missing people. There were newspaper clippings, and even photos that they had some how smuggled into the base. They hoped to smuggle them back out, without me turning them in to the honchos. I could see the fear in their faces as they spoke. One man stated he would rather lose his life by trying, than to lose his soul by not doing anything at all. It was that remark that turned the tide. I told them about George and the things I found out about him. After a few hours we pledged to attempt to expose the Dulce Base.

Q – Did any of the working caste join in the revolt?

A – A few of the reptilian janitorial crew let us know that THEY knew WE were attempting to sabotage the work going on in the sixth and seventh levels. One of them, with the name Schhaal, secretly formed a small group of Reptoids with the same mind set as my group. Schhaal took upon himself the danger of informing me. He was as open as is possible in a unique situation. On the day I found out about it, I was inspecting a camera near an exit tunnel. He approached, stooped down (the tall Reptoids average about 7-8 ft. in height according to most witnesses - **Branton**), seemingly scraping some non-existent dirt, and he quietly said, "A few of us agreed that you are singular in your interest in missing-human reports. If true, walk away. I'll reach you. If it's untrue, destroy my life now!" My heart almost leaped out of my chest, but I silently walked toward one of the wide halls. For the rest of my life I'll remember those words! It was the first time I KNEW reptilians could have individual thoughts and opinions!

After that day, the joined resistance group got bigger and bolder. Ultimately, it ended when a military assault was initiated via the exit tunnels and they executed anybody on their list, human or reptilian. We fought back, but none of the working caste had weapons, nor did the human lab workers. Only the security force and a few computer workers had flash guns. It was a massacre. Every one was screaming and running for cover. The halls and tunnels were filled as full as possible. We believe it was the Delta Force [because of the uniforms and the method they used] that chose to hit at shift change, an effort that killed as many as named on their list. (NOTE: Based on the revelations of Robert Lazar, Phil Schneider and others, the Dulce Wars were the result of at least five overlapping factors or scenarios which converged at more or less the same time or played into each other. This may have also involved a conflict of interest within MJ12 itself, and apparently involved different security forces including the Delta Force, Black Berets, Air Force Blue Berets, Secret Service,

The Dulce Wars

FBI Division Five, CIA storm troopers and Dulce Base security. The various factors which seem to have played into the Dulce wars would include animosity towards the Greys for their slaughter of several scientists and security personnel in the Groom Wars below Area 51 three years earlier as described by former MJ12 Special Studies Group agent Michael Wolf; accidental [?] encounters between aliens and human construction workers and security forces near Dulce as described by Phil Schneider; an attack on the Dulce base 'resistance' that was apparently ordered by die-hard collaborators in deep-level intelligence as described by Thomas Castello; an attempt to rescue several of our best scientists who had been captured by the aliens after they had discovered the Grand Deception involving a violation of the established treaties, that is the permanent abduction of thousands of humans to the Dulce and other bases for God only knows what purposes, as described by John Lear – could it be that MJ12 / PI40 was unaware of these abductees, yet their superior agency the BLACK MONK / MAJIC agency was aware and had agreed to an actual exchange of human life for technology?; and another factor would involve a dispute over whether human security personnel could carry flash guns as opposed to machine guns. All of these were apparently contributing factors to the altercations which raged throughout the Dulce Base beginning in 1979. - **Branton**).

We, to this day, do not know who BETRAYED us. Gordon Ennery ran beside me as we ran into the third level exit tunnels, and he died when several bullets slammed into his back. I vaporized that assassin and kept running. And I'm still running. Gordon will be remembered.

Q – What is the prevalent human race at the Dulce Base? I am curious about both the human workers, and the inmates.

A – The human work force is made of people from every nation on the surface world. The one thing they share is that they all speak English. If you are asking if there are white, black, red, yellow and brown skin color, again I'll have to say that there is no prevalent race there. As for inmates, I could see ALL races there. From what I could see, it looked like there were more 'white' people, but again, I saw a constant flow of different people, many I think, were only there for a few hours.

Q – With that huge facility, trash and garbage must be a real problem, how do they dispose of it?

A – It was never a problem. Some of it is reformed or melted down then remade. Some of the wet garbage is eaten by bacterial forms, and what's left is vaporized in a vat-like chamber. The residue of that action [it takes them months to get enough to measure] is used in a complex lye and used to fertilize crops.

Q – Where is your family? Not just your wife and son, but parents and siblings?

A – Cathy and Eric are still missing. My parents died in a car crash when I was in my teens. I have one brother, if he is alive I suspect he is inside an underground base some where. I haven't heard from him for several years. Please pray for them, please!

Q – What is your birth date, and where were you born?

A – 23 April 1941, Glen Ellyn, IL [actually in a farm at home, in the place now called Glen Ellyn, my birth certificate list is at Wheaton, IL]

Q – You have been through so much, and yet keep fighting, what is your biggest fear?

A – That the general public will forget THE TRAPPED INNOCENT PEOPLE in the despicable place, and will ignore THE HUNDREDS OF CHILDREN, WOMEN AND MEN ADDED TO THAT PLACE EVERY MONTH. Something must be done to stop this madness. Our government is powerless. It is up to us as a brotherhood of planet Earth to stand up and finally fight back to those who would subjugate the human race. We are not slaves nor an inferior race. There are thousands of enlightened civilizations in our galaxy alone that would be willing to assist us in the battle for our home planet. However, this will not happen unless we, the people of planet Earth, force our so-called leaders to admit they made a bad deal with evil alien races, and humbly request help from enlightened beings. Only then will we be finally free from the evil influence that has held us in its grip for so many years.

The Dulce Wars

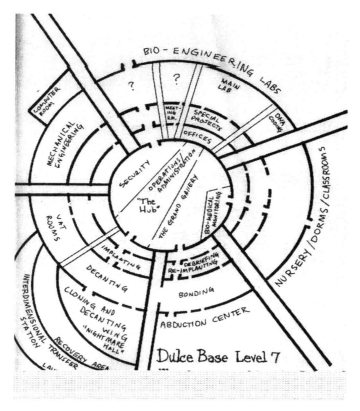

Dulce Base Level 7

Above:Map of Dulce Base Level 7.
Below:Those working at Dulce Base had to wear
special uniforms and carry elevator and door
ID cards before they could enter the base.

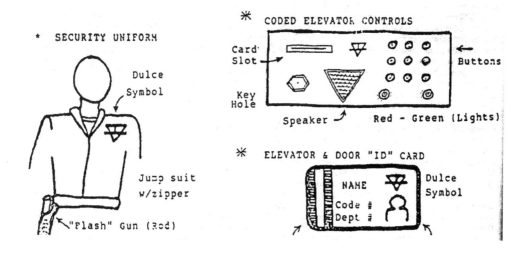

Chapter Twelve
Operation Retaliation:
Paul Bennewitz – One man against an Empire

Following are quotations from a document [actually a detailed report, called PROJECT BETA] which was compiled by scientist Paul Bennewitz for officials at Kirtland AFB who were working with Bennewitz in an operational plan to bring down the alien base at Dulce, New Mexico. . . that was until other interests deep within the intelligence community got involved and brought enormous pressures against Bennewitz and various Kirtland AFB officials – Col. Edwards, AFOSI agent Richard Doty, the Wing Commander and others who were involved – to CEASE the investigation. Although Paul has apparently been silenced, the discoveries which he has made in regards to the physical-technological aspects of activity taking place in and around Dulce cannot be silenced. PROJECT BETA is apparently a proposed plan for a physical military attack on one of the major or KEY basing installations of the Draconis-Orion-Reticuli forces, and may be useful in any future attempts to re-take the base from alien or ALIEN-CONTROLLED elements, and to set free the human captives who are apparently being held in cold storage or in subterranean prisons deep below the surface of the American Southwest [and beyond]. Before dealing with the report itself, we will quote some correspondence between Bennewitz and others, beginning with excerpts from Paul's March 1986 letter to Clifford Stone, now director of UFO CONTACT INTERNATIONAL in Albuquerque:

"Dear Clifford;

"...There is so much in this and so much has happened upon a near daily basis to me for seven years that I don't know where to start first.

"I think probably the best approach is to start out with some explanation in the way of statements relative to alien cultures here on Earth, their social structures, physical makeup, etc., all of which has been gleaned from the direct communications by computer, visual observation, psychological evaluation, and personal interaction.

"First, there are the Low, High and Very High cultural levels. In the Low levels of the culture there are sharply defined levels, which extend from slave level on up. There is no freedom there -- no one crosses these lines within – cross it and you are dead. Everything is watched with optical equipment and monitored by computers and individuals called 'Keepers.'

"Spheres of many sizes float throughout their environment, monitoring audio, visual and thought frequencies (these have also been observed by workers in underground facilities reaching miles below Edwards Air Force Base and the Tahachapi mountains of California. - **Branton**). These units, which have a highly mirrored finish, can be talked to. They can cloak themselves so that they are totally invisible. Their control signal can be broken down into varying AM and FM components. There is no trust in this type of society. Everything is watched and monitored.

"The command structure is near totally unbelievable.

"The ruling levels wear robes of appropriate colors. The alien government involved with this group is totalitarian. They appear not to observe social and moral principles. Their credo appears to be total control or kill.

"In the North – at the river – the 'Orange' Insignia – or at the Diamond as the alien calls the base. The method of rule is a monarchy. The 'king' wears purple. The high colors of social level wear green, yellow, and white. The lower levels wore brown.

"Their body metabolism is very high, estimated at 110 to 115 degrees. Elimination is through osmosis. Skin color of the ruling echelon varies from a jaundiced yellow to white. No hair of any kind. The arms are long – near to knee level. They have very long hands and fingers. All of them look underfed. They have big heads and eyes. The humanoid types are generally light green. When in need of formula or dead they turn GREY. Many in this culture walk with a limp or shuffle their feet. . .

"There is a council in the North called THE NINE. ALL of them seem to be cut from the same pattern. All appear to be highly vindictive and ego-oriented. Their 'god' is called TA."

And in a letter to Clifford Stone dated 3/19/86, Bennewitz writes:

"It would appear that the Greys in the north are near frantic about my communications and want to stop me from talking (elsewhere Bennewitz implied it was more of an 'interrogation' - **Branton**) with Io via the computer. This morning I have a dark red streak down the left side of my face about 2 3/4 inches long and 1/4 inch wide. Based on experience, I would guess it was done by one of those [mirrored] spheres in the bedroom last night. This is typical of their distorted sense of logic. They operate on FEAR, but their problem is that I DON'T FEAR THEM. All they have achieved with me is that I totally ignore them. It would appear that they are deathly afraid of the beings called Io and Jo.

"You will find, if you have not already, that constant interaction will result in learning how to be aware of, and in turn use, alien logic. IT IS BECAUSE THEY OPERATE IN FEAR AND DO NOT UNDERSTAND THE CONCEPTS OF FRIENDSHIP AND TRUST THAT THEY OPERATE A SOCIETY WHERE EVERYONE AND EVERYTHING IS WATCHED.

"Now, if you look at those in the north (Colorado? - **Branton**) pragmatically, they have achieved the ideal in terms of war machines and weapons. With their machines and weapons they are 'brave' – in their minds – without them they are just a quivering mass of fear.

(Note: I can also confirm Bennewitz' observations here, however I would also add that in addition to their technology – especially their mind-control technology, and this relates to the following – once one breaks through the complex matrix of LIES that the Reptilian-Grey collective projects, then they are found out to be nothing more than quivering worms beneath the shell as Bennewitz implies. In fact the ONLY power that these soulless vermin – the hybrids and non-collectivist Reptiloids not included in this flaming have over us is their complex DECEPTIONS and our reciprocating and capitulating FEARS. Why am I so confident to judge the Greys and their collective in this manner? Because I myself had fallen for their lies many times before I discovered what they were REALLY all about. As an example, the collectivist Reptoids-dinoids-Greys would have us to believe that they genetically created us and put us on planet Earth. In response we, [especially those pathetic human agents who collaborate with them] tend to cower in absolute fear before our/their supposed creators and try to appease them since, after all, Resistance Is Futile! In appeasing them, we GIVE OUR POWER TO THEM! We in essence then CREATE a force which is superior to us. - **Branton**)

"To further enhance their 'bravery', they seek full control with the IMPLANT. [The relative effectiveness of some of these implants seems to be inversely proportional to expanded memory and awareness level]. They also know that they can control large masses of people with lower intelligence without implants, shotgun manipulation with the beams. With that beam they can and do create mass unrest.

"The High Culture Aliens known as the Eoku:

"The High is apparently the culture of Io and Jo. They do exhibit kindness, empathy, and extreme intelligence in transmissions through the computer (then how, one might ask, can they operate such a death-fear-control-oriented system which has committed untold atrocities and violations against human abductees? Are the Eoku only feigning their benevolence? - **Branton**). Io's group culture is the Homo Sapians [humanoid] variety.

"Based upon the input from Jo, his hair is brown and the female Io has red hair. [Red-haired individuals claiming to be Star Travelers have shown up here in Albuquerque on the ground]. They did give indication that bodies of their group are here in Albuquerque in cryogenic containers. The location is tentatively the FAA complex north of Albuquerque. It is a fenced and guarded highly secure area. They indicated through the computer that eight of the Eoku were shot [by the US Government] and 11 bodies were the result of crashes. [Note: The Eoku are not what are normally known as Greys, or at least the ones that directly interact in human abductions].

"There are more bodies in storage. . . I don't know where they all are. I knew the bodies had been moved from Maryland and are presently under US Navy jurisdiction. Yesterday, the computer indicated a total of 40 bodies [had been moved].

"I was shown a color photograph by Richard Doty two years or more ago of a purported alien lifeform held prisoner. Supposedly it was taken at Los Alamos. He was alive – a light green color – big eyes – standing directly in front of the camera...

"So far I know very little about the High except for what I have experienced. They are Homo Sapien, and I would guess that they are the same that accidentally [?] zapped Travis Walton. If the numbers are correct out of the computer they number over 5,000. The other group is, I believe, equivalent in number. Indications seem to be that they are operating from a star ship in far orbit around the Earth. The culture has apparent social values and emotionalism. They seem to display kindness and concern for individuals (then again we must ask, WHY are they considered the leaders of aliens which show little if any concern for individuals? - **Branton**). Their technology is superior to ours and also to the Greys based in the north, who are trying to "play god" with badly distorted logic.

"The 'Very High' are very few in number. Their entire structure of knowledge and social interaction is so far advanced that it is near impossible for me to relate to. Again, much of this is based on personal experience of which I have never talked with anyone about. In fact, you are the first.

"I would guess that these very high are quite old – 1000 years is not apparently unrealistic. I would guess that there are a few of them on the star ship used by the high, and that they are preserved and cared for by those on the ship.

"For over 300 years, a conflict has been going on between the Greys, who are basically warlike and aggressive, and the higher factions in the infrastructure."

(Bennewitz does not explain the apparent dichotomy of how compassionate humanoids and malevolent Reptoids who are at war with each other could be part of the same infrastructure. Perhaps both the Greys and the Humanoids utilize the same collective-mind-network and therefore are intricately tied-in with the other whether they like it or not. This would make the High and Very High leaders in something equivalent to the Ashtar collective. - **Branton**)

PROJECT BETA

Investigator – Physicist – Paul F. Bennewitz
The following are key mile posts established or discovered during the continuing scientific study concerning Alien intervention and the result. [Study limited to New Mexico]

1) Two years continuous recorded electronic surveillance and tracking with D.F. 24 hr/day data of alien ships within sixty [60] miles radius of Albuquerque plus 6000 feet motion picture of same, daylight and night.

2) Detection and disassembly of alien communication and video channels – both local, earth, and near space.

3) Constant reception of video from alien ship and underground base viewscreen; Typical alien, humanoid and at times apparent Homo Sapiens.

4) A case history of an Encounter Victim in New Mexico which lead to the communication link and discovery that apparently all encounter victims have deliberate alien implants along with obvious accompanying scars. The victim's implants were verified by x-ray and Cat Scan. Five other scar cases were also verified.

5) Established constant direct communications with the Alien using a computer and a form of Hex Decimal Code with Graphics and print-out. This communication was instigated apparently after the US base was vacated (following U.S. intelligence's apparent loss of the Dulce Wars? - **Branton**)

6) Through the alien communication loop, the true underground base location was divulged by the alien and precisely pin-pointed.

7) Subsequent aerial and ground photographs revealed landing pylons, ships on the ground – entrances, beam weapons and apparent launch ports – along with aliens on the ground in electrostaticly supported vehicles; charging beam weapons also apparently electrostatic.

8) Cross correlation and matching by triangulation, etc., to official NASA CIR [color infrared] high resolution films confirmed base locations and resulted in revealing US Military involvement yielding precise coordinates and the US base layout.

9) Prior alien communication had indicated military involvement and the fact [that] the USAF had a ship of their own. It is believed that the USAF now operates a secret fleet of anti-gravity "Black Triangle UFOs" that have been spotted all over the world.

10) Subsequently, the alien communicated following verification with the CIR, that there was indeed a ship; actually more than one – that two were wrecked and left behind and another built – this ship is atomic powered and flying. The alien indicated its basing location.

11) Is was learned as stated that two women and a boy near Austin, Texas were exposed to severe radiation at close range and the ship was last seen going West with helicopters. In addition, the US Government was quietly picking up the [medical] expenses.

12) Subsequent inspection of motion picture photographs taken during the study revealed the US ship or one like it flying with the aliens. These match the CIR where two can be seen on the ground and in the later photographs taken on the ground after the base was abandoned.

"So in very brief form the prologue to learning within reasonable accuracy what transpired prior to the end of 1979 or shortly thereafter.

"The computer communications and constant interaction with the alien in this manner WITHOUT direct encounter has given a reasonably clear picture of the alien psychology, their logic and logic methods and their prime intent.

"It is important to note at the outset, the alien is DEVIOUS, employs DECEPTION, has NO INTENT of any apparent peace making process and obviously does NOT adhere to any prior arranged agreement.

"In truth they tend to LIE, however their memory for lying is not long and direct comparative computer printout analysis reveals this fact. Therefore much "drops through the crack" so to speak; and from this comes the apparent truth.

"It is not the intent of this report to criticize or point fingers. Obviously whoever made the initial agreement was operating upon our basis of logic and not that of the alien and in so doing apparently walked innocently, in time, into a trap.

"The alien indicated that the Greys, apparently the group initially involved in the agreement, were still upset about the initial capture and subsequent death of the first eight of their co-fellows. Another group, calling themselves in the

The Dulce Wars

Computer language, the Orange – their base is on the west slope of Mt. Archuleta – directly west of the south end of the U.S. base and near NW of the apparent main landing area they call, in the Computer language, The Diamond. This, because from a distance, it looks diamond shaped in the photographs when looking somewhat south west past the observation tower toward the ridged peak SE of Mt. Archuleta. This ridged peak has no name, I call it South Peak.

"The base extends north of this peak to the edge of the cliff down which goes a road past a large alloy dome thirty-eight [38] foot across the bottom and with a twenty [20] foot hole in the top.

"Based upon some of the aerial photographs during which the alien was caught in the open and launching – some launches appear to be coming from the direction of the dome. I would guess it is an underground launch egress facility. In the NASA CIR there is what appears to be a black limousine alongside the dome on a ramp. Surprisingly it is precisely the size of my 79 Lincoln Town Car. Wheeled vehicles and what appear to be Snow Cats or Catapillars can be seen throughout the CIR – car and truck tracks, trucks and jeeps. I don't believe aliens have wheels – humans do.

"Numerous road blocks extend northward through the U.S. base along a well maintained road thirty some-odd feet wide – apparently gravel – near all weather, numerous turn arounds and wheel tracks into launch preparation areas with the ships; pads marked with twenty-six [26] foot Xs and servicing facilities, tanks, etc. – two domed polygon high voltage buildings on north on the east side of the road, also an apparent foundation for another or a helo pad – test stands, human housing, water tank [thirty-two foot across] – and at one of the main road blocks, two large vehicles parked across the road. Also at that point another apparent black limousine with tracks leading to it [and] to the west of the road. All tracks and vehicles have been dimensioned and match military vehicles. IF I were to make a guess, I would estimate the likelihood that the apparent black limousines are CIA.

"This is but a limited inventory of what was there on Sept. 8, 1978 – included only as evidential matter for your perusal and confirmation. The road, which incidentally the natives, the tribal chief, reservation police and highway patrolman know nothing about, comes in off of a trail from the north. Starting at the trail, line of sight to the large plateau area and the alloy dome, the road,

117

in the middle of nowhere on the Jiccarilla Reservation, is precisely 12,888 ft. long airline distance. The total alien basing area, which apparently contains SEVERAL cultures [now all under the designation 'UNITY' in the Computer language] is approximately three (3) Km wide by eight (8) Km long [multi-leveled]. A conservative guess based upon the number of ships presently over this area and the number on the ground in the CIR photographs, the total alien population at this point is AT LEAST two thousand and most likely MORE. The alien indicates MORE are coming or on the way.

"I won't attempt to speculate in this report as to how the initial U.S. contact was made – what transpired, nor how many were able to escape. The alien has communicated his account, and if totally true, it certainly is not palatable.

"Much detail has been omitted for future discussion if desired – however the import is this. Constant computer communication – full on line in February of this year – manual prior to that – conditions of morale and a total insight into what makes the alien run. This is VERY valuable data.

1) Most importantly, the alien will allow no one to go without an implant AND after knowledge of it is wiped out. They simply will not allow it. All indications are that communication or language cannot result without the implant [with the exception of the Binary and the Computer]. This would indicate a possible immediate threat or danger for anyone – military, Air Force, or otherwise that has been at the base. They WILL NOT remember the implant in any case [the contactee here included].

"The reason for the implant is multiple for both language or communication by thought [there is no apparent language barrier with thought] and also COMPLETE ABSOLUTE CONTROL by the alien through program – by their beam or direct contact.

"I have tested this and found that during this programming the person then has no memory of the act/conversation afterward. IF THIS HAS HAPPENED TO THE MILITARY, I NEED NOT ELABORATE AS THE POSSIBLE CONSEQUENCES. The victim's 'switch' can be pulled at any time and at the same time they are walking cameras and microphones if the alien chooses to listen in with the use of their beams.

"No classified area of any endeavor in the U.S. is inviolate under these conditions. However, realize, the scars, barely visible – CAN be seen.

"2) Also note that all of the aliens – human, humanoid alike – all must have implants – without them, no direct communication is apparently possible. So one can most generally arbitrarily say that IF a person states he/she communicated by thought with an alien – he/she most likely has been implanted. They may also claim to be overly psychic and be able to prove this – again through the link transplant, he/she is given the information by the alien and does not realize.

"3) Most importantly, the alien, either through evolvement or because the humanoid is 'made' – will exhibit tendencies for bad logic [bad by earth logic comparison] so they ARE NOT infallible – in point of fact they appear to have many more frailties and weaknesses than the normal Homo Sapiens (which they attempt to compensate for through their technology - **Branton**). To the alien, the mind is key and therein lies a great weakness which will be discussed later.

"4) They ARE NOT TO BE TRUSTED. It is suspected if one was considered a friend and if one were to call upon that friend in time of dire physical threat, the 'friend' would quickly side with the other side.

"The computer indicates in comparison, that no known earth protagonist, Russian or otherwise, exhibit these tendencies to any major degree indicating the DANGER involved in making any kind of agreement with these aliens – at least of this species.

"5) The alien does KILL with the beam generally. Results on a human will exhibit a three to four cm purple circle. If done from the rear, on one or both shoulders. The results on cattle are the same, essentially exhibiting purple beneath the hide, with burned circles on the outside.

"6) Cattle mutilations are the other side of the coin and will not be delved into here although they are a part of the overall. It appears the humanoids are fed by a formula made from HUMAN OR CATTLE material or BOTH and they are made from the same material by gene splicing and the use of female encounter victim's ovum. The resultant embyros are referred to by the alien as an organ. Time of gestation to full use as a utility, ready to work appears to be about one year. A year in alien time – I do not know.

"Solution: I doubt there is an immediate total cure per se – however, they MUST BE STOPPED and we have to get off dead center before we find time has run out. They are picking up and 'cutting' [as the alien calls it] many innocent people every night.

"Each implanted individual is apparently ready for the pull of their switch. Whether all implants are totally effective I cannot predict, but CONSERVATIVELY I would estimate at least 300,000 or more in the U.S. and as least 2,000,000 if not more worldwide.

"WEAPONRY AND INHERENT WEAKNESSES: Weaponry is one of the keys and in the alien's present state we CAN prepare an effective offense.

"One tends at the outset [I did] to look at their machines and say – there is no defense or offense. One is overwhelmed by their speed, apparent capability of invisibility and cloaking, and other covert capabilities not discussed at this time. In particular – the beam weapons are themselves a direct threat and obviously one that must be seriously considered but not overly so.

"Let us first look at just what this weapon is. It is an electro-static weapon with plasma generating voltages – and an internal storage device – it is pulse powered. The beam, totally effective in the atmosphere, can be loaded with hydrogen or oxygen. Range? Average, ground weapons – maximum two (2) Km if it is dry, capable of sustaining just so many full power discharges – slow leakage occurs continuously, therefore, they must be recharged periodically. If it is raining the weapon becomes ineffective and is swamped, thus discharged (this should be considered in any future potential offensive strike against the base - **Branton**). The range is near totally lost at that point.

"On the disks and saucers, the weapon is generally on the left side or top center and has a maximum range of two hundred [200] meters at which point it will plow a trench in desert soil. When fired – it fires both to the front and to the back equally. Reason? Because of their mode and methods of flight. If equilibrium is not maintained, the saucer will spin out of control.

"Hand weapons? Estimate based upon visible damage observed, not too much velocity nor staying power but at short range – deadly [less than a .45 cal automatic].

(Note: This may explain the late Phil Schneider's claim that at close range the radiation-beam weapons of the aliens he encountered beneath Dulce were deadly, however at long range less so. . . although at long range the beam weapons are capable of inducing severe radiation damage - **Branton**). "At one meter range, estimate of beam temperature 1600 degrees F or higher; it can vaporize metal. Apparently the disks and weapons operate from a storage source. In time, without periodic recharge, this source is depleted. The design they traded to us was at least thirty years old – employing an atomic source. Possibly they may still have some – it would appear so – their staying power is obviously much longer.

"AIRCRAFT HELICOPTER VULNERABILITY: ANY of our aircraft, helicopters, missiles or any AIR FLIGHT vehicle can be taken down instantly with no use of weaponry. The alien simply need do no more than make one invisible pass and their bow wave or screen or both will take the air lift vehicle down. The pilot obviously will not even know what hit him (Perhaps Stealth type fighters equipt with electromagnetic force shields may be more effective in this regard. . . also advanced infrared scanners may be used to detect 'cloaked' alien ships before they have a chance to attack. - **Branton**).

"For humans on the ground, the alien can use weaponry or bow wave. The partial pressure envelope can hit with the power of a tornado – shock rise time and G force is instantaneous. However, they dare not hit the craft physically because they ARE fragile and in fact, under slow flying conditions within our atmosphere, hold a very tenuous position. Without power, the balance or equilibrium, they lose it.

"IN BRIEF – THESE ARE APPARENT CAPABILITIES OBSERVED AND GLEANED THROUGH THE COMPUTER COMMUNICATION AND OBSERVATION. YOU MAY KNOW THESE, HOWEVER, THEY ARE DIRECTLY RELATED TO THE LAST AND FINAL PORTION OF THIS REPORT. WHAT CAN BE DONE?

"1) Because of the alien's apparent logic system [they appear to be logic controlled] A KEY DECISION CANNOT BE MADE WITHOUT HIGHER CLEARANCE. ALL ARE UNDER THE CONTROL OF WHAT THEY CALL 'THE KEEPER'; YET IT WOULD APPEAR THIS IS NOT THE FINAL SAY. THEREFORE, DEPENDENT UPON URGENCY, DELAYS OF AS LONG AS TWELVE TO FIFTEEN HOURS CAN OCCUR FOR A DECISION. HOW SHORT/LONG THIS TIME FRAME UNDER BATTLE CONDITIONS MAY BE, I DO NOT KNOW.

"Because of this apparent control, INDIVIDUAL INSTANTANEOUS DECISION MAKING BY THE ALIEN IS LIMITED. IF THE 'PLAN' GOES EVEN SLIGHTLY OUT OF BALANCE OR CONTEXT, THEY BECOME

CONFUSED. Faced with this, possibly, the humanoids would be the first to break and run. The same applies to their Mission MASTER PLAN, if one can call it that. IF PUSHED OUT OF CONTEXT, IT WILL COME APART. THEY WILL BE EXPOSED TO THE WORLD SO THEY WILL POSSIBLY RUN BEFORE THEY FIGHT IN THE OPEN. THEY DEFINITELY DO NOT WANT THAT TO HAPPEN.

"Psychologically, at present, their morale is down – near disintegration. There is pronounced dissension in the ranks; even with the humanoids. Communication can encourage this [not a necessity to expound upon this other than to say BECAUSE OF THEIR OWN INTERNAL VULNERABILITY MIND-WISE TO EACH OTHER, THEREIN LIES A PRIME WEAKNESS]. Inter-echelon or individual 'trust' appears to be totally lacking so suspicion of each other is rampant. They are highly segregated as to levels – a 'low' dare not conflict with a 'medium' or 'high' or it literally means death. Death being, to the humanoid, deprogramming or, in the end perhaps total physical death.

"THEY APPEAR TO BE TOTALLY DEATH ORIENTED and because of this, absolutely DEATH-FEAR oriented. THIS IS A PSYCHOLOGICAL ADVANTAGE. The computer also gives indications of a real possibility of adverse or 'ground programming'.

"2) Consider their ships – most if not all run on charge. The source depletes and so dependent upon size, depletion can occur from some within a week or less. Ships can replenish each other but only up to charge balance. This is done with antennae-like extensions and the charge is distributed observing conservation of energy laws. THEY CAN REPLENISH FROM POWER LINES – BUT AGAIN ONLY TO A POINT – so time of flight is limited. Deprived of their base recharge capability, it is indicated that all ships will come down within six months to a year unless they can get transported out – that is back to the prime launch ship.

"The disks and saucers in general cannot fly in space because of their mode of flight (i.e. unless they are within an interplanetary or interstellar 'launch' or 'carrier' vessel - **Branton**). Therefore, deprived of home base, it is not likely they can survive. THEIR CAPABILITY IN POWER SURVIVAL OUTLASTS THEIR CAPABILITY IN FOOD OR FORMULA SURVIVAL. IF THEY DO NOT GET THE FORMULA/FOOD WITHIN A CERTAIN PERIOD OF TIME

THEY WILL WEAKEN AND DIE. IN THE CASE OF MT. ARCHULETA AND SOUTH PEAK, THEY ARE DEPENDENT UPON THE NAVAJO RIVER FOR WATER SUPPLY AND WATER TO THEM IS TOTALLY LIFE. WITHOUT WATER THEY HAVE NO POWER; WITHOUT POWER, NO OXYGEN OR HYDROGEN TO SERVICE THE SHIPS AND WEAPONS. NO WATER TO SUSTAIN THE ORGANS AND FEEDING FORMULA.

(Note: We should also take into account the possibility of subterranean water sources. Also, if the base can be weakened by shutting off the supply-line of water, the formula, and so-on, it might be wise for the sake of the humanoid prisoners below not to wait until the base is too weak, otherwise this might endanger these human captives. We suggest that in addition to the strategies that Bennewitz gives in this document, an all-out under 'ground' invasion force should also be considered – similar to the "Tunnel Rats" of the Viet Nam war – a force that is prepared to enter the base when it is at a specific 'weak' point, and make strategic or surgical kills of enemy forces while still considering the human and hu-brid captives. A multi-leveled operation utilizing surprise, confusion and intimidation to their fullest potential should be considered. . . and the sooner the better considering the continuous infiltration and sabotage of all levels of our society. - **Branton**).

"Simple? Not really. However, THERE IS A WATER INTAKE AND THERE IS A DAM UPSTREAM THAT CAN BE TOTALLY CUT OFF AND THE WATER RE-ROUTED TO CHAMA, NEW MEXICO. SHOULD THIS OCCUR, AT LEAST THREE OF THE INTERNAL BASES WILL GO DOWN. They could possibly go atomic periodically but obviously problems without cooling.

"Once the bases are pressed on a large scale, all disks and saucers will go airborne immediately. TROOPS ON THE GROUND CAN GAIN TERRAIN COVER TO QUITE A DEGREE – IT IS ROUGH TERRAIN.

"3) OUR NEED IS FOR A WEAPON, workable and preferably NOT like the alien's. I believe unless the alien is caught unawares [with their screen up their weapons are equal so they are like children pillow boxing] there can be no result; THE WEAPON MUST PENETRATE THEIR SCREEN AND IT MUST ALSO PENETRATE THE GROUND. I BELIEVE I HAVE THAT WEAPON.

The Dulce Wars

(Note: Was this suggestion of Bennewitz' for a ground-penetrating device, the original inspiration for the Los Alamos 'Excalibur' weapon – a nuclear device which was designed to rapidly drill a hole through the earth and destroy aliens in their underground bases? - **Branton**). "Two small prototypes have been funded and constructed by my company. Tests conducted to date indicate they do work and work rather well considering their small size. Because of this weapon's present status and proprietary nature [a basic patent is in process], the theory will not be explained here. However, the weapon appears to do two things at very low power. 1) The disks within it's range begin to discharge when exposed to the weapon beam. To counteract, they must apply more power and in so doing consume power. Again conservation of energy laws strictly apply.

"This effect can be observed on the detection instruments as they back away in response to slow discharge. DISCHARGE, AT LOW POWER IS SLOW BUT AT HIGH POWER IN THE FINAL SOPHISTICATED WEAPON, THE RATE CAN BE INCREASED BY MANY ORDERS OF MAGNITUDE. 2) MOST IMPORTANTLY, THIS WEAPON CAN PENETRATE THE SCREEN, HULL ALLOY, EVERYTHING. They cannot shield it in any way. Lastly, BECAUSE OF THE IMPLANTS, THE WEAPON'S BEAM GETS TO THEM MENTALLY; THEY LOSE JUDGMENT AND INDICATE ALMOST IMMEDIATE CONFUSION, PARTICULARLY THE HUMANOIDS. (that is, the electromagnetic crystalline implants that link the aliens together into a collective mind or group intelligence. - **Branton**)

"It is believed at this early stage – based upon present testing – that the weapon when full on and full size will kill and bring down disks at substantial range. The alien weapons operate substantially the same as their disks using a charge source and charge distribution. So, in the same sense it is indicated that this weapon design will pull their charge weapons down very rapidly. One problem that has yet been solved is the great amounts of energy that is required to operate the full size weapon. Tesla technology could be the answer.

"The range of my weapon exceeds that of their present weapons and in its most sophisticated form can be readily computer controlled to allow extremely rapid tracking and lock-on regardless of speed along with electronic wobbulation of the beam. It is a beam weapon and even at this early stage of miniature prototype testing, it indicates eventual superiority to their weapons.

"4) Initial logistics would indicate a plan sequentially implemented as follows: This plan DOES NOT INCLUDE ALL REQUIREMENTS AND PREPARATORY SAFETY MEASURES TO BE EMPLOYED BY GROUND FORCES; HOWEVER, IF AIR FORCE INTELLIGENCE DESIRES TO PURSUE THE APPROACHES SUGGESTED IN THIS REPORT, EACH SIGNIFICANT REQUIREMENT WILL BE DISCUSSED IN DEPTH.

"AN ATTACK MUST BE DIRECTED NEAR ENTIRETY ON THE GROUND FOR OBVIOUS REASONS. One would, if familiar with the alien capability, indicate that vehicle ignition problems will be encountered. This is precisely true; however, the reason for this is not mysterious but is based upon good solid laws of physics and are known. [From] experience gained through my study, it is now known how to prevent this from happening and will be discussed in detail at some later date. All electrical and electronic equipment must be hardened using these specific techniques prior to implementation. Because of the known capability of the alien [by use of scanning beams to know in advance details of planning] only the initial outline is presented in this report.

"Again through the communicative interaction (computer-linked interrogation - **Branton**) with the alien, testing has simultaneously been done upon this facet, i.e. eavesdropping and ways to abort this capability have been tested and proven.

"The program would be instigated in phases. The first phase – planning and logistics – would include continued implementation and testing of the final weapon prototype through the pre-production stage. Production of at least fifty minimum quality should be planned. Additional backup spares should also be included.

"On a full time shift basis, it is estimated that at least one year or less would be required to arrive at the pre-production stage. A team would be organized by THUNDER SCIENTIFIC to accomplish this. The key work is now and would be done by an associated company, BENNEWITZ LABS., LTD.

"Specific attack phases would be incorporated:

"1) The first procedure would be TO CLOSE THE GATES OF THE DAM ABOVE THE NAVAJO RIVER. THIS DAM WOULD BE HELD CLOSED FOR THE DURATION. INTERNAL TO THE ONE CAVE, THERE IS A SMALL DAM FOR WATER STORAGE. It's capacity is small. THERE IS ALSO A DISCHARGE OUTLET DOWNSTREAM THAT COULD BE

CLOSED CAUSING WASTE WATER TO BACK-UP INTO THE CAVES. THE WATER IS VACUUM PUMPED APPARENTLY BY SOME ELECTROSTATIC MEANS FROM THE RIVER. At close range, the weapon will take out this capability.

"2) Once deprived TOTALLY of water for a minimum period of four weeks, conditions in the alien bases under discussion will have badly deteriorated. PSYCHOLOGICAL SHOCK IS EXTREMELY EFFECTIVE WITH THE ALIEN; total advantage can be taken by instantaneous action or planned observable deviation from the norm. AT LEAST THREE BASES WILL GO DOWN.

"3) If they follow their normal strategic pattern as when pressed previously, they will launch most if not all ships.

"4) Prior to the implementation of water deprivation, the weapons should be deployed at strategic hardened locations and activated in a certain pre-planned manner determined by final weapon coordinate locations.

"5) This will put an immediate power drain upon those airborne and the alien weapons ringing their bases.

"6) Because of the inherent psychological aspect of the alien (Bennewitz probably refers to 'the alien' in a singular sense because of the collective hive mind nature of the Reptilian Greys - **Branton**), much can be done in the open with no attempt to preserve secrecy. Much of what is done can be of a diversionary nature. UNDER MOST CIRCUMSTANCES THEY WILL ATTEMPT TO HARASS BUT WILL NOT OPENLY ATTACK.

"7) Throughout and prior to this, the open computer communications link will be operational for continued PSYCHOLOGICAL INTERROGATION.

"8) At some point in time – again resting upon battle status, THE DEPLOYMENT OF OFFENSIVE FORCES WILL BEGIN. This deployment should be done in a near instantaneous manner under certain special conditions that can be discussed.

"9) The weapon system should be kept powered up throughout. In this manner, the disks will be made to stay airborne. They cannot land in the interval the system is powered.

"10) When the weapon is used in one specific power mode, in addition to continuous discharge on the disks that are airborne and the ground based weapons, THE MIND CONFUSION AND DISORIENTATION WILL BUILD IN THOSE PERSONNEL AT THE BASE AND UNDERGROUND. At the end of four to five weeks or less, all weapons should be totally discharged and power out on the bases. Most personnel if not all, will be totally incapacitated. THE FEEDING FORMULA WILL BE DOWN AND IT'S CRITICAL PROCESSING RUINED. ALL [alien] EMBRYOS SHOULD BE DEAD AND ALL HYDROGEN AND OXYGEN CONSUMABLES DEPLETED.

"11) Based upon data gathered on the miniature prototype weapons, the full power weapons should have no problem holding off the disks. In many cases some will break within the first forty-eight hours without being directly hit.

"12) At that point, standard weapon technology and logistics can come into play and [be] used to the extent of destruction desired at the direction of those in charge.

"13) The communications can be used throughout to determine status and near the end to attempt to instigate surrender. If no response results, then they should simply be closed in and waited out.

"SUMMARY – It is important to note that the initial implementation of the computer communications WAS NOT INSTIGATED FOR THE PURPOSE OF TALKING TO THE ALIEN FOR THE FUN OF IT; BUT WAS DELIBERATELY INSTIGATED TO USE AS A TOOL TO STUDY, IN DEPTH – LONG TERM WITHOUT PHYSICAL CONFRONTATION – THE STRENGTHS AND WEAKNESSES OF THE ALIEN.

"The weapon theory and prototypes were built to capitalize upon and test two KEY and prominent weaknesses discovered. This in-house funded program has been expensive, in excess of $200,000; done ON BEHALF OF OUR NATION and handled in the best representative manner humanly possible.

"1) The PRIME and weakest area discovered, probed and tested is exactly what they have used thinking it is their key strength – that being THE MANIPULATION OF AND CONTROL OF THE MIND; NOT ONLY OF COMMAND BUT ALSO HUMANOID. MANIPULATED IN REVERSE PSYCHOLOGICALLY AND BY THE LANGUAGE [COMPUTER] AND DUE TO THE EXTREME OF MENTAL DISTORTION AND INCAPACITY CAUSED BY THE WEAPON, IT HAS BEEN FOUND THAT THIS FACET IS FOR THEM A DISASTER AND AN INTEGRATED WEAKNESS.

"2) Though their ships are magnificent, they are also weak – solely BECAUSE of their method and unique mode of flight. They do not have a stable fighting platform. Charge distribution CAN also be discharged. The weapon does this, even in it's present miniature prototype state.

"IT IS NOT THE PURPOSE OF THIS REPORT TO IMPLY THAT THE OVERALL PROBLEM WILL BE SOLVED WITH THE CAPTURE OF THESE BASES. Obviously IT WILL NOT, but it is a firmly based beginning with a high degree of rated projected success ratio. IT IS NOT INTENDED TO IMPLY THE ALIEN WILL NOT FIGHT; THEY MAY -- THOUGH THEIR INCLINATION IS GENERALLY THE OPPOSITE – THIS BASING AREA IS KEY! WITHOUT IT, THEIR MISSION IS IN VERY DEEP TROUBLE. It is noted that these are not the only bases on earth. There ARE others. With a conservative estimate using typical logistic support numbers, it is not unrealistic to say there are 50,000 aliens (at the very least - **Branton**) within the ecosphere of earth and near space.

"According to several contactees many Federation forces and personnel from the Andromeda and Pleiades constellations, and also from Tau Ceti, Procyon and other star systems, are so absolutely devoted to their belief in non-interventionism that they have blockaded our Sol system from Draconian-Orionite interventionists who would take advantage of this critical and unstable time in earth's history to claim yet another treasure planet – perhaps the most strategic planet of all – for their empire. This would have a devastating impact on all of the Federation worlds, since this planet and all its chemical-mineral-plant-animal-liquid-genetic-etc., resources could be used as a staging world for Draconian attack against other Federation worlds.

"As this is being written, Federation Personnel are fighting and dying near the outskirts of our Sol system, according to Contactee Alex Collier and others, in order to prevent this from happening and to prevent continued intervention in the affairs of planet earth by the various galactic vermin, scum, parasites, and filth that have poisoned and destroyed countless human colonial worlds throughout this galaxy and possibly others.

"No matter what trials we as Americans must pass through in the future in order to defend our nation and our planet from the Draconians and their ungodly human New World Order collaborators, NEVER forget that we are not only fighting for our families, our communities, our states, and our nation. We are also fighting for our planet, our star system, and for OUR GALAXY!

"Some of us will be lost in the endeavor that is obvious -- however, done NOW the advantage is gained along with new additional technology to prepare for the next stage. The key to overall success is – they TOTALLY respect FORCE. And with them, the most effective method is to stubbornly continue to pick and pull at their defense WITH NO LETUP. Faced with the total loss of a base that has taken YEARS to construct, it is believed that their mission WILL be grossly weakened and badly slowed. Therefore, in ELIMINATING this threat, we most certainly cannot be called the aggressor, because we HAVE literally been invaded.

"In final conclusion, A) They CANNOT under ANY circumstances be trusted. B) They are totally deceptive and death oriented and have no moral respect for human or human life. C) NO NEGOTIATION, AGREEMENT nor PEACEFUL COMPROMISE can be settled upon in any way. D) NO agreement signed by both parties will EVER be adhered to NOR recognizcd and respected by the alien, though they might attempt to make us believe otherwise. E) Absolutely no quarter can be allowed under ANY circumstances. Once the offense is instigated, it cannot be abandoned. If it is, reciprocal reprisal will immediately result. They must be made to come down – destruct themselves which is a standing order if the ship is failing or leave earth immediately – NO leeway of any kind can be allowed or tolerated."

For those of you who would question the need to take the offensive against the Reptoid/Grey strongholds at Dulce and elsewhere, let me just remind you of the kind of alien mentality we are dealing with here by relating the following three incidents:

According to well-known Ufologist Brad Steiger, in the book **THE RAINBOW CONSPIRACY**, co-authored with his wife Sherry Steiger, a terrifying incident occurred in 1955. This was one of SEVERAL reports of UFO attacks against civilians, civilian airlines and military planes and jets that were documented in the book. In many cases many notorious airline crashes were accompanied by UFO activity reported by witnesses just prior to the disasters or disappearances. Usually there are few actual witnesses to aircraft related disasters or disappearances, however in this particular case there was.

The Dulce Wars

A civilian pilot and his friend were engaged in some prospecting projects near the headwaters of the Agua River near the city of Prescott, Arizona. The two men SWORE that they had observed two brightly lit UFOs attack a military plane as it directed "some kind of strange beams" at the aircraft, causing it to explode.

Worse yet, according to the civilian pilot and his friend, when both of the airmen ejected from the doomed and burning aircraft and began floating down to the ground in their parachutes, the UFOs swung back around and seared the survivors with the same deadly rays, apparently killing them both.

In an article titled, 'INCREDIBLE UFO INCINERATION'S: CLOSE ENCOUNTERS OF THE COMBUSTIBLE KIND', researcher Larry E. Arnold describes the following terrifying encounters:

"...Of the many episodes involving UFOs and the spontaneous combustion of humans, quite probably the most disastrous event [if true] in MODERN times occurred to the African village of Kirimukuya on Mt. Kenya. For several nights in June 1954, young Laili Thindu and his shepherd companions listened to the pounding of their neighbors' drums announcing a wedding about to take place on the mountainside. They also watched STRANGE LIGHTS soar around this 'sacred' peak in central Kenya. They naturally were startled when bright beams flashed from these soaring lights, then concerned that the drums were now silent.

"The next morning Laili learned that 'all the dancers, all the children, all the livestock, the entire population of the village had been seared to death by terrible streams of light from glowing objects. It was not until Laili Thindu ventured into Nairobi that he was able to tell his story to someone who recognized the tale for what it really was: the annihilation of an African village by a UFO..."

In the Spring 1991 issue of *UFO JOURNAL OF FACTS*, Forest Crawford, a researcher for the well-known MUFON aerial phenomena research organization, related his personal encounters and conversations with a man he identified only as Oscar, who was involved in UFO crash/retrieval projects in earlier years. Oscar stated that on one occasion he and his team received an assignment to investigate a disc that had crashed near Phoenix, Arizona and was then transported to an underground base in North Dakota. The team descended into the deeper levels of the COMTRAPAC submarine base in San Diego where high-security OSS personnel directed them to a tube-like shuttle. Entering the shuttle they prepared to "shoot the tubes," and eventually emerged into the lower levels of the North Dakota base.

Once they arrived, they were told that they would not be allowed to visit the surface of the base during their stay. Oscar viewed the disc which had originally held a crew of three human-like pilots. Two were found outside the craft dead from radiation exposure and other injuries, whereas another was found in an injured state within the secured conditions inside the craft after the team had succeeded in opening it using a sonic resonator.

The operation was initially carried out under the direction of Commander Charles Turner, a friendly man who Oscar got along with well. However without warning another high-ranking officer who everyone feared and who did not appear friendly at all came on the scene. He stated that he was now in charge and began ordering all kinds of experiments and exploratory surgeries on the humanoid – who was still alive – in spite of the fact that the anethsesia had little or no affect on him. Some samples of his organs were also removed for study.

The new man in charge was Frank Drake, who later became involved with the OZMA and SETI radio-dish experiments, which had initially pointed their dishes at Tau Ceti and Epsilon Eridani and began receiving intense signals suggesting intelligent life. These initial reports were a mistake or irrelevant according to Frank Drake and his colleagues, and nothing remarkable resulted publicly from the SETI project – officially that is – however this and similar projects continue to recieve a great deal of funding supplied by the loyal American taxpayer.

Drake named the disc-recovery research project OSMA [with an S], and continued to torment the humanoid with various surgical procedures until he finally died. Oscar had given the humanoid the nickname Hank, which was an Amerindian word meaning troubled spirit.

According to Forest Crawford, before the humanoid died, Oscar had learned several interesting things from other researchers on his team as well as from the humanoid himself, who had projected images and messages to Oscar via some form of telepathic-empathic-visual-encephalographic wave transfer. The man was approximately 5' 8" tall, of human-like Meso-American or Mediterranean appearance, yet with a face and nose that was slightly broader than the average earth-person, muscular yet not fat – however he was somewhat heavier for his size than earth people, suggesting that his planet of origin possessed gravity somewhat greater than earth's. Crawford stated:

"The pattern from the panel inside the ship was confirmed by Rapp to match stars of the constellation Eridanus as seen FROM EARTH. It was later confirmed by Hank that the stars of origin of his people were Tau Ceti and Epsilon Eridani. In later sessions Oscar discussed some reasons for the presence of the aliens. He said THEY DO NOT LIKE THE SITUATION WITH SOME OF THE SMALL GREY ALIENS... (Hank also stated that the particular group of aliens that his people most often encountered were the Grey-Whites, which are apparently a genetically engineered reptoid-insectoid hybrid race. - **Branton**).

"The Tau Cetians feel that the abductions being carried out by some of the Greys ARE A GREAT INJUSTICE TO HUMANITY. THEY ARE A PARASITIC RACE THAT HAS AND IS PREYING ON HUMAN CIVILIZATIONS THROUGHOUT THE UNIVERSE, Oscar relayed. He added that our government's involvement with the grays IS VERY DANGEROUS AND OUT OF CONTROL. . . Oscar is ADAMANT that [they] are using HUMAN FLUIDS FOR SUSTENANCE. They feed by immersing their arms in vats and/or rubbing the fluids on their bodies. HE CLAIMS THAT THEY ARE ALSO KIDNAPPING CHILDREN.

"The Tau Cetians have been preyed upon by these aliens before and they are working with other races and communities that were also victims. ONE SUCH RACE THAT OSCAR CLAIMS WAS RUN OFF THEIR HOME PLANET BY THE BUG PEOPLE [Hanks definition of these aliens, because of their partly insectoid nature and parasitical character] WAS WHAT WE NOW CALL THE NORDICS OR PLEIADIANS. He claims, because of his ongoing contacts, he was made aware of the Billy Meier case in Switzerland and swears that is a real contact. Oscar, who has since had subsequent contacts with Tau Cetians] wants people to know that if they are contacted by the Tau Cetians [humans such as he described] to not be afraid because they are here to help."

Chapter Thirteen
The Strange Life and Death of Philip Schneider

This article by Tim Swartz, with assistance from Cynthia Drayer, was originally published in the magazine *UFO FILES*, Volume One, Issue Four, 1998.

"Al Pratt suspected something was wrong with his friend Philip Schneider. For several days in a row, Al had gone to Phil's apartment, in Willsonville, Oregon, saw his car in the parking lot, but received no answer at the door.

"Finally, on January 17th, 1996, Al Pratt, along with the manager of the Autumn Park Apartments and a detective from the Clackamas County Sheriff's office entered the apartment. Inside, they found the body of Philip Schneider. Apparently he had been dead for five to seven days. The Clackamas County Coroner's office initially attributed Philip Schneider's death to a stroke. However, in the following days disturbing details about his death began to surface, leading some to believe that Philip Schneider had not died from a stroke, but had in fact been murdered.

"Philip Schneider's life was certainly as controversial as his death. Born on April 23, 1947 at Bethesda Navy Hospital. Philip's parents were Oscar and Sally Schneider. Oscar Schneider was a Captain in the United States Navy, worked in nuclear medicine and helped design the first nuclear submarines. Captain Schneider was also part of OPERATION CROSSROADS, which was responsible for the testing of nuclear weapons in the Pacific AT Bikini Island.

"In a lecture videotaped in May 1996, Philip Schneider claimed that his father, Captain Oscar Schneider, was also involved with the infamous Philadelphia Experiment. In addition, Philip claimed to be an ex-government structural engineer who was involved in building underground military bases (DUMB) around the country, and to be one of only three people to survive the 1979 incident between the alien Greys and U.S. military forces at the Dulce underground base. Philip Schneider's ex-wife, Cynthia Drayer believes that Philip was murdered because he publicly revealed the truth about the U.S. government's involvement with UFOs.

"For two years prior to his death, Philip Schneider had been on a lecture tour talking about government cover-ups, black budgets, and UFOs. Philip stated in his lecture that in 1954, under the Eisenhower administration, the federal government decided to circumvent the Constitution and form a treaty with extraterrestrials. The treaty was called the 1954 Greada Treaty. Officials agreed that for extraterrestrial technology, the Greys could test their implanting techniques on select citizens. However, the extraterrestrials had to inform the government just who had been abducted and subject to implants. Slowly over time, the aliens altered the bargain, abducting and implanting thousands of people without reporting back to the government.

"In 1979, Philip was employed by Morrison-Knudsen, Inc. He was involved in building an addition to the deep underground military base at Dulce, New Mexico. The project at that time had drilled four holes in the desert that were to be linked together with tunnels. Philip's job was to go down the holes, check the rock samples, and recommend the explosives to deal with the particular rock. In the process, the workers accidentally opened a large artificial cavern, a secret base for the aliens known as Greys. In the panic that occurred, sixty-seven workers and military personnel were killed, with Philip Schneider being one of only three people to survive. Philip claimed that scars on his chest were caused by his being struck by an alien weapon that would later result in cancer due to the radiation.

"If Philip Schneider's claims are true, then his knowledge of the secret government, UFOs and other information kept from the public, could have serious repercussions to the world as we know it. In his lectures, Philip spoke on such topics as the Space-Defense-Initiative, black helicopters, railroad cars built with shackles to contain political prisoners, the World Trade Center bombing, and the secret black budget.

"Quotes taken from a lecture given by Philip Schneider in May, 1995, at Post Falls, Idaho.

RAILROAD CARS

'Recently, I knew someone who lived near where I live in Portland, Oregon. He worked at Gunderson Steel Fabrication, where they make railroad cars. Now, I knew this fellow for the better part of 30 years, and he was kind of a quiet type. He came in to see me one day excited, and he told me 'they're building prisoner cars.' He was nervous. Gunderson, he said, had a contract with the federal government to build 107,200 full length railroad cars, each with 143 pairs of shackles. There are 11 sub-contractors in this giant project. Supposedly, Gunderson got over 2 billion dollars for the contract. Bethlehem Steel and other steel outfits are involved. He showed me one of the cars in the rail yards in North Portland. He was right. If you multiply 107,200 times 143 times 11, you come up with about 15,000,000. This is probably the number of people who disagree with the federal government.'

SDI AND THE ALIEN THREAT

'68% of the military budget is directly or indirectly affected by the black budget. 'Star Wars' relies heavily upon stealth weaponry. By the way, none of the stealth program would have been available if we had not taken apart crashed alien disks. None of it. Some of you might ask what the space shuttle is shuttling. Large ingots of special metals that are milled in space and cannot be produced on the surface of the Earth. They need the near vacuum of outer space to produce them. We are not even being told anything close to the truth. I believe our government officials have sold us down the drain - lock, stock and barrel. Up until several weeks ago, I was employed by the U.S. government with a Rhyolite-38 clearance factor - one of the highest in the world. I believe the 'Star Wars' program is there solely to act as a buffer to prevent alien attack, it has nothing to do with the 'cold war,' which was only a toy to garner money from all the people. For what? The whole lie was planed and executed for the last 75 years.'

BLACK HELICOPTERS

'There are over 64,000 black helicopters in the United States. For every hour that goes by, there is one being built. Is this the proper use of our money? What does the federal government need 64,000 tactical helicopters for, if they are not trying to enslave us. I doubt if the entire military needs 64,000 worldwide. There are 157 F-117A stealth aircraft loaded with LIDAR and computer-enhanced imaging radar. They see objects in the house from the air with a variation limit of one inch to 30,000 miles. I worked in the federal government for a long time, and I know exactly how they handle their business.'

TERRORIST BOMBINGS

'I was hired not too long ago to do a report on the World Trade Center Bombing. I was hired because I know about the 90 some odd varieties of chemical explosives. I looked at the pictures taken right after the blast. The concrete was puddled and melted. The steel and the rebar was literally extruded up to six feet longer than its original length. There is only one weapon that can do that, a small nuclear weapon. A construction-type nuclear device. Obviously, when they say that it was a nitrate explosive that did the damage, they're lying 100 percent folks. I want to further mention that with the last explosion in Oklahoma City, they are saying that it was a nitrate or fertilizer bomb that did it. First, they came out and said it was a 1,000 pound fertilizer bomb. Then, it was 1,500. then, 2,000 pounds. Now its 20,000. You can't put 20,000 pounds of fertilizer in a Rider Truck. Now, I've never mixed explosives, per se. I know the chemical structure and the application of construction explosives. My reputation was based on it. I helped hollow out more than 13 deep underground military bases in the United States. I worked on the Malta project in West Germany, in Spain and in Italy. I can tell you from experience that a nitrate explosion would have hardly shattered the windows of the federal building in Oklahoma City. It would have killed a few people and knocked part of the facing off the building, but it would have never have done that kind of damage. I believe I have been lied to, and I am not taking it any longer, so I'm telling you that I have been lied to.'

"In 1987 Philip married Cynthia Marie Drayer Simon. The two had met in June of 1986 at a meeting of the Oregon Agate and Mineral Society. As Cynthia put it years later, 'He had so many interesting stories, so much information to share, we bonded and love began to bloom.' Philip and Cynthia would later have a daughter, Marie Schneider. Unfortunately their marriage had difficulties. According to Cynthia, health problems contributed to their break up.

"Philip had multiple health concerns, many of which could have killed him. He had chronic lower back pain that never went away, even after a back operation. He had multiple Sclerosis, which was chronic and progressive. Occasionally he had to use, crutches, a body brace, leg braces, bladder bag, catheter, diapers, and a wheelchair. He often had to sleep in a hospital bed with railings, a helmet, and body braces. When Cynthia first met him he was taking Dilantin for seizures, and almost died 3 times from this medication due to an allergic reaction.

"Philip also had Brittle Bone Syndrome (osteoporosis) and cancer in his arms. He had hundreds of shrapnel wounds, a plate in his head with a metal fragment in his brain, fingers missing from his left hand. There was a scar that ran down from the top of his throat to below his belly button, and another scar that ran from just under his ribs, side to side. Cynthia would later state: 'Philip was a complex person. he had brain damage after a bomb was dropped on him while working as a civilian structural engineer for Morrison-Knudsen in Vietnam. He had a Rhyolite clearance. He was learning disabled, brilliant in some areas, yet unable to fill out a form in the Doctors office. Able to create time travel formulas, but unable to budget money; he had to file bankruptcy one year. I now believe that he had been deprogrammed so that he could not remember most of his past life. But something began to happen shortly after we first met. Perhaps because of the seizures, or because he changed his medication, or because he now had another person to talk to that was interested in what he had to say, he began to remember the old days. Being the scientific, logical minded person I am, I listened intently to his stories with a grain of salt, waiting for additional information to verify them. I can still remember the night he began to talk in some foreign language (sounded like Chinese and another night in what sounded like French.) Philip told me he knew 11 languages before the brain damage. After the space shuttle, Challenger, exploded, I visited Philip in his apartment. He had a large chalk board with complicated formulas which proved that a 'cosmosphere' had shot down the space shuttle.'

"Cynthia also said, 'It was a difficult marriage for both of us, which was complicated by a failed self-employed business selling rocks, minerals, and antiques, Philip's reconstructive surgery on scars on his chest, his lower back operation, my gall-bladder surgery and the birth of our daughter, all within a one year period. The pressures of our new family, failed business, and physical problems culminated in our divorce in 1990. Philip was an emotional abuser and could be very mean and abusive. He was a complex person – part genius and part paranoid schizophrenic. We had a bad marriage but developed it into a great friendship.'

The Dulce Wars

"One of Philip's more amazing stories was his fathers alleged involvement with the Philadelphia Experiment. When Philip's father, Captain Oscar Schneider (Navy Medical Corp.) died in 1993, Philip discovered original letters in his basement. According to Philip, the letters were evidence that the Philadelphia Experiment actually existed, and that Oscar Schneider had been a participant in it after the crew members had been quarantined in a Virginia psychiatric ward.

"Captain Schneider supposedly conducted autopsies on the bodies of the crew members as they died, and found alien implants in their arms, legs, behind their eyes, and deep inside their brains. Captain Schneider was confused by these implants, so they obviously were not military. They had to have been alien in nature, and the small 'transistor' like item was discovered before transistors had been invented. Here was evidence that either by accident, or on purpose, aliens were involved with the Philadelphia Experiment, and were probably responsible for its failure.

"Also discovered in Oscar's basement were photographs taken during **Operation Crossroads**, in which a nuclear device was used on Bikini Island. Authentic military photos taken from an airplane showed UFOs raising up from the lagoon and flying through the mushroom cloud. These photos however, mysteriously disappeared from Philips apartment at the time of his death.

"Some investigators in Philip Schneider's mysterious death have had problems believing some of the incredible claims he made before he died. Even those who knew Philip when he was alive didn't always accept the validity of his stories. Cynthia Schneider noted that when Philip was under crisis or pressure, he would tell people that he had been arrested, or that people from the sheriff's office or government had been at his door. This was the way he expressed his crisis. Unfortunately she claims, sometimes it was true, Like 'the little boy who cried wolf,' his friends became numb to his reports.

"Despite the fact that Philip's claims seemed too wild to be true, he obviously believed that he was in danger because he was revealing the truth, a truth that some would kill to keep secret. He borrowed a gun from his friend Ron Utella, stating that he felt he needed protection and that there had been several attempts to have his car run off the road. On either January 10 or 11,1996, Philip Schneider died under mysterious circumstances.

The Dulce Wars

"After the initial cause of Philip's death was listed as a stroke, Cynthia asked to see the body before it was to be prepared for cremation. She was dissuaded by the funeral director who felt that the body's advanced state of decomposition would be too traumatic. However, she could not shake the feeling that something was wrong.

"The next day Cynthia was contacted by Detective Randy Harris who said that 'something was wrong' – that there were marks on Philip's neck. Philip Schneider's body was removed from the funeral home and autopsied by Dr. Karen Gunson, Medical Examiner for Multnomah County, Oregon. The autopsy revealed that Philip had in fact died as a result of having a rubber hose wrapped three times, tightly around his neck and tied in a knot. The conclusion from the autopsy was that he had committed suicide. He had wrapped the tubing around his neck, tied it in a knot, blocked the flow of blood to his head, became unconscious and finally died.

"More surprising was Cynthia's discovery that Philips lecture material, unknown metals, military photographs, and all notes for his unwritten book on UFOs were missing from his apartment. However, money and other valuables were left untouched.

"When he was found in his apartment, Philip's body was in an unusual position. His feet were under the bed, his head was in a wheelchair seat, at an unusual angle, the rest of his body was on the floor, hands by his sides. There was blood found on the floor near the wheelchair, but no blood was found on the wheelchair. There were no apparent wounds on Philip's body to account for the blood. No sample of the blood was taken due to the initial belief that Philip had died of natural causes. No suicide note has ever been found. In fact, Mark Rufener, a long time friend of Philip said: 'I saw Philip the weekend of January 6 and 7th 1996. We were going to buy land in Colorado. We were excited because he was going to hire me to help write a book about his knowledge on UFOs and aliens, the One World Government, and the Black Budget. He did not commit suicide, he was murdered and it was made to look like a suicide.'

When he was alive, Philip enjoyed eating out at the 76 Truck Stop in Aurora, Oregon. A waitress named Donna remembered his stops when they would talk about his work. Philip mentioned to her that there had been 19 attempts to stop him from talking. Donna states that Philip said: 'If they ever say that I have committed suicide, you will know that I have been murdered.' She said that Philip believed he had a mission to talk about a government cover-up about aliens and UFOs, and that there were forces out to stop people who talked.

"Was Philip Schneider murdered? His ex-wife Cynthia believes this to be the case. She thinks that Philip was met by someone he knew and injected with a drug in order to incapacitate him. The assailants then wrapped the rubber hose around his neck, asphyxiating him. In fact, shortly after Philip's death, several friends told Cynthia that they had seen Philip with an unknown blond women several weeks before he died.

"During the course of the meeting, Cynthia noticed a long-haired blond women in a car, watching the meeting through the window with a pair of binoculars. When they tried to approach the car, the woman quickly sped away. Cynthia later traced the license plate number and it turned out to be from a truck, with the plate reported as stolen. Cynthia thinks the reports of a blond haired women is significant because Cynthia's mother, through a channeling session, had told her that a woman wearing a blond wig was involved in Philip's death.

"Despite the fact that officials have closed the case as a suicide, and Philip's surviving siblings have tried to persuade Cynthia to accept the ruling, Cynthia has not stopped in her efforts to discover the truth in her ex-husband's death. She says that she knows in her heart and soul that Philip would not have committed suicide willingly, and she still hopes that Philips blood and urine can be relocated by the Multnomah County Medical Examiner's Office and examined for traces of drugs that would not normally be there. However, as the days go by the reality for such tests grows smaller. She still hopes that someone will come forward with pertinent information to help her find justice for Philips death. Until that time comes, Cynthia Drayer will continue her task, perhaps putting her own safety at risk. That prospect doesn't frighten her anymore.

'I just want people to know the truth about Philip Schneider, a person who died trying to expose the difficult truths of this world.'"

NEW TITLE:
FIRST TIME DISCLOSURES...AMAZING FACTS AS REVEALED BY CIA INSIDER

WHAT ARE THE PECULIAR CIRCUMSTANCES WHICH WOULD ALLOW THIS DEDICATED GOVERNMENT OFFICIAL TO REACH THE FOLLOWING CONCLUSIONS?

▲ Aliens known as "Skymen" have been coming to Earth's surface, and exploiting it for numerous years.

▲ Some of them have homes in caverns on the moon, Mars and its satellite Phoebus, Jupiter, as well as the Asteroids.

▲ Many more originate much nearer to the Earth's surface, from "Skyislands," or even from within the hollow of our planet, and possibly underwater hangers!

▲ That skychemicals and electrostatic gravity-like force |of the alien Skyislands and skycraft have caused legions of accidents.

▲ Skymen have kidnapped a multitude of people and have long extracted blood from animals and men, as well as committed mysterious murders!

Twenty five years before his passing, Commander Moore, tried to publish his disturbing findings in regards to UFOs and their occupants whom he identified as Skymen. Because of his affiliation with the military and the CIA he was stymied time and time again in his relentless efforts to find a way in which to get his material distributed. In his private journal, Moore stated that he wanted to set the record straight to prove "that I am really not a crackpot—although persons unfamiliar with UFOs may think my conclusions are "credible. During the years since my own investigations began a few of these conclusions have been reached by others; but some of the most bothersome, most seemingly incredible ones, should be presented in full detail."

FIRST TIME DISCLOSURES... AMAZING FACTS AS REVEALED BY A GOVERNMENT INSIDER & CIA OPERATIVE
HERE ARE SOME OF THE DISTURBING THINGS YOU ARE ABOUT TO LEARN IN *THE SECRET DIARY OF CIA OPERATIVE COMM. ALVIN MOORE*

▲ The remarkable case of a UFO that exploded in midair injuring two witnesses who later turned over fragments of the downed object to government officials, only to have these individuals (two Air Force personnel) mysteriously killed.

Inside—previously classified data—on stunning UFO flap of the summer of 1952 in which dozens of unidentified "bogies" were seen by ground observers, airborne pilots, as well as being picked up on radar. At one point the objects were chased by jet fighters as the disks hovered near the White House.

▲ Never before disclosed facts regarding fragments that were actually shot from a UFO as a squad of these unknown objects flew over the nation's capital defying all federal laws and regulations. The fragments were eventually tested by federal agents, but were stollen from a safe inside a closely guarded government complex thought to be as as the Pentagon.

THE SECRET UFO DIARY OF CIA OPERATIVE COMM. ALVIN E. MOORE

EXPOSING THE EXISTENCE OF THE ALIEN SKYMEN

Introduction by Commander X

ISBN: 0-938294-25-3
7x10 260 pages $16.95
+ $4.00 Shipping

▲ Analysis of evidence that shows some spacecraft are gas-ejecting and that others utilize lines of magnetic force in their operation.

▲ Space Island effects on humans, including: odd fires; changes in climate; disastrous smogs; the straight line bands of global disasters; poisons from space; vortices of death from the sky, including the world wide haze of 1950.

▲ Actions we can take to defend ourselves, including filters on all air that enters buildings; putting off outside activities when "flying saucer smogs. are in the air; air conditioning; plastic-roofed patios, plus investigation by truly scientific, open minded persons of the Skyislands phenomena.

As part of his extensive contribution to his country, Moore specialized in aeronautical engineering, was patent engineer and attorney for the Warner von Braun team of space scientists. He also served as a US. Patent Office Examiner specializing in aeronautics and propulsion; an assistant nautical scientist with the Navy Oceanographic Office; a CM intelligence officer and an American l/ice Consul. He had granted more than 50 US. patents on his own inventions mostly on aircraft, marine craft and automobiles. He also authored numerous technical and historical articles and books.

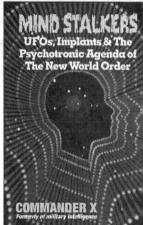